REGAINING CONTROL OF YOUR LIFE

REGAINING CONTROL OF YOUR LIFE

JUDSON EDWARDS

BETHANY HOUSE PUBLISHERS
MINNEAPOLIS, MINNESOTA 55438
A Division of Bethany Fellowship, Inc.

Published by Bethany House Publishers
A Division of Bethany Fellowship, Inc.
6820 Auto Club Road, Minneapolis, Minnesota 55438

Printed in the United States of America

Library of Congress Cataloging-in-Publication Data

Edwards, Judson.
    Regaining Control of Your Life / Judson Edwards.
      p.   cm.

    1. Christian life—Baptist authors.
2. Stress (Psychology)—Religious aspects—Christianity. I. Title.
BV4501.2.E3156   1989
248.4'86132—dc 19   88–32773
ISBN 1-55661-053-X   CIP

To the guy from Lake Wobegon
and all of us
who are just like him

JUDSON EDWARDS is the pastor of Heritage Park Baptist Church in Houston, Texas. He obtained a B.A. in religion from Baylor University and an M.Div. in theology from the Southwestern Baptist Theological Seminary. As an author, he has written four other books: *A Matter of Choice, Running the Race, With Love, From Dad,* and *Dancing to Zion.*

CONTENTS

INTRODUCTION

In *Lake Wobegon Days*, Garrison Keillor has one of his characters confess, "I find it very hard to whoop it up, hail a pal, split a gut, cut a rug, have a ball, or make a joyful noise." Sadly, many of us are in the same boat, becalmed and wishing we could catch a swell once in a while.

Yesterday, as I was checking out at a local convenience store, the young woman at the cash register asked sweetly, "Aren't we going to smile today?"

"Maybe later," I snapped curtly. *Who does she think she is anyway?* I wondered, snatching my bag from her hand. *I don't look* that *gloomy. I just look like my normal self.*

Later, I got to thinking, *Maybe that's the problem. My normal self looks pretty gloomy.*

I am not by nature a jolly good fellow. I am the shy, nervous type that likes solitude and privacy. Give me a choice between a crowd and a good book, and I will always choose the latter. No one has ever accused me of being the life of any party.

My idea of a good time is running three miles a day in the Texas heat. While normal people are eating chips and dip, and watching a ball game on television in an air-conditioned living room, I am jogging through the subdivision, panting and sweating with glee.

Predictable. That's me. I feel certain my children will remember me best for two questions I constantly ask them: "Did you brush your teeth?" and "Have you cleaned your room?" In my thinking, cleanliness is next to godliness when it comes to teeth and bedrooms.

You get the picture. I tend to be a circumspect, anti-septic party-pooper. I preach joy better than I live it. Indeed, I write about the abundant life better than I live it, too.

For some time now, I've struggled with being an uptight Christian. I've discovered, for one thing, that my uptight-ness is usually my own fault, that I've created much of the stress in my life. But I'm getting better.

I am gradually learning to loosen up, to laugh, to experience grace first-hand. I am learning to smile politely at check-out girls, to party, to eat chips and dip, and to let my kids be human. And I'm learning that if God is *for* me, who or what can possibly be against me?

I hope that in writing of my discoveries, I can help you unwind, too.

I dedicate this book, then, to me, and to the guy in Lake Wobegon, and to all Christians everywhere who are just like us. May we all learn, before we arrive at eternity's party, how to whoop it up a little.

I am come that they might have life, and that they might have it more abundantly.

John 10:10 (KJV)

"I'm going to start out by assuming that you are approximately as unhappy as I am. Neither of us may be submitting ourselves to psychiatrists, neither of us may take an excessive number of tranquilizers each day, neither of us may have married three times in an effort to find someone to make us happier. We are not (quite yet) desperate, but we are, vaguely, dissatisfied. . . ."

Walter Kerr, *The Decline of Pleasure*

1

THE CASE OF THE UPTIGHT CHRISTIAN

*H*elen is a fine woman. Ask all who know her and they will tell you she's the epitome of virtue. She has a happy marriage and three well-adjusted children. She has taught Sunday school at her church for years, and is past-president of the women's mission group. No doubt, Helen is an upright woman.

But those who know her best and love her the most would confide, if pressed, that she is also an *uptight* woman. The older Helen grows the more nervous she's become. She's been known to spew anger like a volcano spews fiery lava when her husband is late from work or her children have a poor showing on their report cards. In spite of all her Sunday school rhetoric about "the abundant life," Helen knows deep inside that she is not experiencing it.

When her pastor preached on joy one recent Sunday, she cynically dubbed him "a pious dreamer." She wished it were true, but in the "real world" of the suburban housewife, she had not found much joy.

Later, in a rare moment of candor, she told one of her friends, "I'm a little ragged around the edges, and I honestly don't know how to turn things around."

Randy is an engineer, a father, and a lay leader at church. His friends and family all say, "Give Randy a job and you can sit back and relax. He'll do a first-class job. The man's a self-starter and a go-getter."

And so he is. His father preached to him, "Anything worth doing is worth doing right." And Randy took the message to heart.

But his wife and kids have noticed a splinter of irritability poking out of his demeanor. He gets testy when things don't go his way around the house, and his teenaged daughter has said at least a dozen times in the last month, "What *is* it with Dad?" Randy's blood pressure has inched steadily upward and, occasionally, he gets a burning feeling in his chest that causes him concern. He has scheduled a visit to the doctor next month.

Randy knows his faith in God is supposed to guarantee him peace—"the peace that passes all understanding"—but worry dogs him daily. Worry about his job. Worry about the kids. Worry about things he can't verbalize to anyone. Sometimes he prays that God will remove the load, but so far his prayers have bumped the ceiling and fallen helplessly at his feet. . . .

Examples of the Ordinary

Helen and Randy are not unusual. Their anxiety, their struggles, their secret hopes are common to most of us. In today's world, stress is a given. To dream of a totally stress-free existence is to dream a fantasy that, at least this side of heaven, just will not be. We are trapped, like Helen and Randy, in homes, jobs, and a culture that naturally produces stress. And I'm sure you have, at times, wondered how to go about "regaining control of your life."

Occasionally, I fabricate a world free of pressure. . . . *In my fantasy world, I sip coffee on the back porch of my Texas*

12

ranch home and gaze at my Hereford cows down by the pond. I make my living cranking out books full of wisdom and style that are eagerly awaited by millions of readers. All is gladness and light, with never a churning stomach or tension headache . . . Then I snap to and face the latest stack of bills.

It doesn't hurt to escape to a fantasy world every now and then—as long as we know it *is* a fantasy. My *real* world contains grumpy people, boring committee meetings, Sundays when I have little to say but have to preach anyway, children who don't respect the sanctity of my afternoon naps, and the tedium of job routine. No wonder my fantasy world is so enticing!

I have a hunch, though, that even if I did write best-selling books from the ranch house, I would not escape stress. I would still have to read the horrors in the morning newspaper, struggle to be a worthy husband and father, cope with an assortment of physical aches and pains, and balance the checkbook every month. In short, though it makes me wince to admit it, even my fantasy world would not be stress-free. Nor would yours.

Someone has compiled a list of the major stresses human beings might face in a lifetime and assigned a corresponding rating to each stress. The death of a spouse, the death of a child, the loss of a job, and other possible stresses are listed and assigned a number.

Obviously, any one of those events would engender a tremendous amount of pressure and grief. In fact, I have no quarrel with the list's compiler. Yet I also know that little, seemingly insignificant events create stress, too. A look of anger from a husband or wife, a quarrel with an adolescent child, getting snubbed when the pay raises are handed out at work, a series of obscene phone calls in the middle of the night—these events cannot be calibrated on a stress scale, but they are stress-makers nonetheless.

There is no shortage of stress-makers in the real world. The rapid pace of modern life intensifies stress till it becomes like slow, silent, physical torture. Everything from headaches to heart failure is now blamed on stress. Experts in both medicine and psychology agree that an antidote for stress would greatly reduce the hospital population. And all the while our society simmers with a collective steam that threatens us all.

The Good News About Stress

The silver lining in this otherwise suffocating cloud is that stress is not necessarily evil. *Too much* stress cripples us. The *wrong kind* of stress chokes our joy. But stress in moderation is actually beneficial. Stress expert Hans Selye has coined a special term—"eustress"—to describe those stresses we experience that are positive and life-enriching.

We have learned, for example, that we must have stress if our bodies are to stay healthy. The old law of physics asserted that a body at rest tends to stay at rest. Man has learned through experience, though, that a body at rest also tends to grow flabby and useless! We actually have to create stress for our bodies if they are to function properly. The runner intentionally stresses his heart every time he jogs his miles. The weight lifter purposely stresses her muscles every time she works out. Health enthusiasts know that apart from stress, physical conditioning is impossible. And the same principle applies to our emotions and our spirit.

My idyllic existence on the ranch (assuming my books sold well, and the kids behaved, and no disease attacked the cows, and on and on ad nauseam) would be a pleasant one. But that pressure-free environment might not be as conducive to my emotional and spiritual growth as my current situation.

Moderate stress prods us to change and nudges us toward newness. Dr. George Sheehan captures this positive aspect of stress when he writes in *This Running Life*, "We need to feel danger, chase after conflict, seek stress. Our aim is a sound mind in a sound body. Stress is simply the resistance we encounter in seeking that health for our body and truth for our soul."

Certainly, the kind of pressure we're discussing in this book is not this positive pressure that nurtures. We will always live with some tension, and can learn to be grateful for some of it. What we *can* try to shed are those unnecessary, negative pressures that rob our enthusiasm and make the promise of abundant life sound like a pipedream.

Misery As a Favorite Pastime

The shocking, ironic thing about most negative stress is that it is self-induced. Most of us have a special knack for adding unnecessary stress to our lives. All the time we are buying books on happiness and earnestly beseeching God for joy, we are living in destructive, stress-producing ways. Tragically, we pray for peace and, at the same time, live in such a way as to guarantee havoc. When it comes to joyful living, our right hand seldom knows what our left hand is up to.

A little further in this book, I'm going to address some of our "great expectations"—those false lines we've drawn on our maps that lead us away from joy. But here, at the outset, let's consider some common myths that make us uptight.

Ten Myths of Uptight Christianity

1. God will love me more if I *do* more. (Truth: God loves me completely right now. All of the sweat-soaked piety and goodness I can muster cannot add one jot or tittle to His love.)

2. It is more Christian to work than to play. (Truth: The truest test of our faith is our capacity to laugh, to treasure life, and to celebrate God's goodness.)

3. I can't make any mistakes because the world is watch-

15

ing my witness. (Truth: It is a serious mistake to think I will never make a mistake and a presumptuous mistake to think the world is particularly interested in my life.)

4. I am the only Bible some people will ever read. (Truth: God is at work in the world, and if by some strange, unforeseen chance I should pass from the scene, He will be able to manage without me.)

5. Morality is the heart of the Christian message. (Truth: Grace is the heart of the Christian message.)

6. On my deathbed I will be sorry I didn't accomplish more. (Truth: If I have time at all for regrets, I will be sorry I didn't love more lavishly and enjoy life more fully.)

7. Most Christians (including myself) are lazy and un-committed. (Truth: Most Christians [including myself] are burned out and disillusioned.)

8. Most Christians (including myself) need to learn the value of hard work and dogged determination. (Truth: Most Christians [including myself] need to learn to relax and experience joy.)

9. It is wrong and self-centered to concentrate on my joy. (Truth: Joy is one of the proofs of the presence of God in my life.)

10. Life is grim business, and I must treat it seriously. (Truth: Life is a holy gift full of exciting possibilities, and I must live in constant gratitude for it.)

I say it again for emphasis: Much of our misery is self-inflicted. That *sounds* like bad news, but that premise actually holds a concealed promise. For if *we* create many of our stresses, that means *we* are in control of them. What we create, in other words, we can *un*-create. We are not ragdolls at the mercy of demonic pressures over which we have no power. And if we have chosen to live in ways that induce stress, we can also choose to live in ways that open the wells of inner peace. Our stress, to a great extent, lies in our own hands.

Here's the dividing line: Until we realize that most stress is a choice, we will never know that we can cross over

16

and move toward inner peace. We will quietly curse our fate, pine for a better job, yearn for a more understanding family, and become more and more miserable as the days go by. As long as we think all stress comes from "out there," we will make little effort to deal with it. Why battle the inevitable?

Go ahead—admit that much of your tension is self-induced. Have the courage to confess that you've succumbed to destructive, joy-killing patterns of living—even as a "good Christian"! Admit your part in the crime, and thus accept your part in the rehabilitation. Then you're ready to take the first step toward joy.

A "Primer" of Hope

I grew up on a steady diet of Isa. 26:3: "Thou wilt keep him in perfect peace, whose mind is stayed on thee: because he trusteth in thee" (KJV). That was my father's favorite verse, so I learned it early and used it often. When threatened with normal boyhood fears—school tests, a big ball game, neighborhood bullies—I would pull out Isa. 26:3 and assure myself the situation was now in my hip pocket—or God's—or *someone's*! That verse was my amulet, and it warded off many an evil spirit.

As I grew older, though, I realized that quoting that verse and living it were worlds apart. As my stresses increased, mumbling Isaiah's promise didn't always still my pounding heart. Getting the truth of that verse from my confident brain to my wobbly knees didn't always work! And it still doesn't. It's made me wonder what the prophet really meant.

"Staying" our minds on God does not mean we withdraw from the real world and take up permanent residence in the prayer closet. It means, rather, that we live in the real world with our lives centered on Him. We live as if God matters. We *trust* in Him.

I want you to recognize that peace has a price tag. Peace

comes to those who build their lives around the ways of God. To put it bluntly, we reap what we sow. If we sow foolishly, we reap a crop of frazzled nerves. If we sow wisely, we grow perfect peace.

That means there is hope for the harried! All of the Helens and Randys of the world can take heart. If they will begin *now* to drop some new seed into the soil, they will eventually produce a different harvest. They will move from self-induced stress to self-induced peace.

Naturally, we would like to find an easy answer to our dilemma. We desire a miraculous, pain-free remedy that will soothe our spirits (like the magic salve that purportedly dissolves inches of fat while we sleep). Of course, we can get quick relief from the *effects* of stress. A tranquilizer, a seminar, a book, or a vacation will do the trick—for a while. But eventually we have to face up to the *source* of the pain. A quick treatment of the *symptoms* is not the same as looking long and hard at our lives and rooting out the *causes* of our stress.

What I hope to do is to help you uncover the ways you produce unnecessary stress for yourself. We're going to rummage around and find destructive behaviors and ideas, then set about removing them. Replace the old, bad seed with a new and better variety, if you will.

As with all seeds, the seed we plant today will not bloom overnight. We're not looking for a "quickie" solution, but a healthy, steady way of living that leads to peace. And we can be confident that good seed will eventually come to fruition.

Peace will not come with pills and programs, but with a style of living that is patiently and carefully cut from a biblical pattern.

How Strong Is Your Heart?

A sign on the Alaska Highway reads, "Choose your rut carefully. You'll be in it for the next two hundred miles."

Most of us have chosen our ruts carefully and been in them for years. Getting out of them will not be easy. Habits die hard.

Change will not come easy for anyone who has become—dare I suggest it?—addicted to stress. When we take stock of our lives and try to deal with our growing misery, we have to make some painful decisions.

Our upright-and-uptight Helen may have to resolve that:

- I am too critical of those around me and will have to loosen up a bit.
- My husband will never be the "Mr. Perfect" I expect him to be. I'm going to love him as he is.
- My children are not brilliant and will probably never be the scholars I want them to be. I will have to accept them as they are and look for other ways to affirm them.
- I've become self-absorbed and need to look for ways to get involved with others.
- My cynicism about the Christian life is not my pastor's fault, or my family's fault, or God's fault. I've built my life on some false premises and need to plant some different seed in my life.
- I've become too private and introspective. I must find someone with whom I can be honest.

And Randy, should he gather his courage and look his stress in the eye, will have to make similarly hard resolutions about the direction he's going:

- I'm too concerned about my image. I need to learn to relax and be myself.
- I've been living as if money is more important than my family. I've got some serious priority shifting to do.
- My body is telling me something about my spirit. My physical ailments are signaling a sickness of the soul.
- I've arrived at mid-life without a true friend in the world. Unless I turn things around, I will die with dozens of acquaintances and not one person who really loves me for who I am.

- My faith is not really mine. Most of what I believe I've never examined. It's time to find some bedrock essentials on which I can build my life.

If Helen and Randy arrive at those conclusions, they are rare people, indeed. Most people will never have the courage to challenge the status quo, even if that status quo is one of boredom and misery. Making those kinds of changes is just too hard for some folks.

Though we Christians like to think we are "open" and "free," the truth is most of us abhor change. I want to warn you that we will be looking at core issues of our lives—such as how we spend our money, how we relate to people, how we relate to God, how we handle our guilt. Each upcoming chapter will probe a sensitive spot and seek to show how our distorted thinking in that area produces unnecessary stress.

The journey to inner peace, then, is for the strong of heart. Timid searchers need not embark on the trip. If we're afraid to look honestly at who we are and how we've bungled our lives, we might as well buy a lifetime supply of tranquilizers and plan on making them a major part of our diet. It takes courage to find personal peace.

The Secret You Already Know

Actually, I am banking on the fact that you already know the road to peace—that it has just been covered over by years of inattentiveness. I hope not so much to teach you new truths, but to jog your memory.

When the singer completes her concert and then agrees to do one more song for an encore, which tune does the crowd want? Some new one never heard before? Not a chance! They'll always clamor for an old song, the singer's trademark, the one everybody has heard a thousand times.

Our hearts have sung to us a thousand times how to live joyfully, how to experience perfect peace—because that is what the heart desires more than anything else. If we had any sense at all, we would listen gladly and hear our heart's music. We would ask it for encore after encore and thrill to its melody.

But, *amazingly,* we don't. We listen to the men at the office or the ladies at the bridge club. We read books on success and write letters to advice columnists. We fall into step with everyone else and assume *they* will lead us to joy. But just take a look around: the crowd is headed for frenzy.

I hope this book will help you listen to God's quiet voice. Peace is the song He sings. I want to help you learn to sing that song again.

For Reflection and Discussion

1. Do you identify with Helen and Randy in this chapter? Would you call yourself an uptight Christian?

2. Do you ever dream of a world free of pressure? Where do you go in your fantasy world?

3. Do you agree that most of the stress we have is self-inflicted? Are there some self-inflicted stresses you can pinpoint right now?

4. Reread the Beatitudes (Matt. 5:1–12) and ponder Jesus' strange words about happiness. Let them remind you that Jesus' idea of happiness is far different than the current one.

5. Circle where you would put yourself on a "life satisfaction" scale.

1	2	3	4	5	6	7	8	9	10

    Very miserable   Very satisfied

6. Are most people really unwilling to change? Are *you* willing to examine your life and make some changes?

Do not conform any longer to the pattern of this world, but be transformed by the renewing of your mind. . . .

Romans 12:2

"To live by expert advice is to abandon one's life."

Wendell Berry, *The Unsettling of America*

2

READING THE WRONG DIRECTIONS

*A*ll of the modern "isms" that were supposed to take us to inner peace—materialism, hedonism, "me"-ism, activism, and all the rest—only lead to grief. This much is clear: Only those who are "different" will find peace. That is, only those obstinate in their particularity can hope to latch on to joy.

You can verify this truth in one of two ways. First, you can try the popular, well-traveled road and learn firsthand it is a dead end. You can enter the rat race, climb the ladders, scratch the backs, make the investments, join the clubs, polish the apples and discover for yourself if you find joy. Our world is littered with disillusioned, "successful" people who have gained the whole world and inadvertently lost their soul.

Or you can verify the futility of the "broad way" by just being observant. Cast a discerning eye at the people you know. How many of them have perfect peace? How many exude a contagious joy? How many are living abundantly?

Whether we learn it by experience or observation, it is becoming more apparent that only nonconformists, only people who will dare to travel a lonely road, have a chance at peace. The accepted program for success has produced a society of uptight, downcast people.

A Trio of Nonconformists

We shouldn't be surprised—not if we have listened to wise voices from ages past. Wise men throughout the centuries have observed with Soren Kierkegaard that "the crowd is untruth."

Take the Preacher in Ecclesiastes, for instance. He set out to follow the recommended recipe for the good life. Amazingly, that recipe was about the same when the Preacher lived 2,300 years ago as it is today. The Preacher pursued knowledge and "madness" and "folly." He built an impressive house, planted vineyards, stockpiled silver and gold. He worked diligently, had plenty to eat and drink, and bathed himself with luxury and pleasure. In short, he was a success. Or was he? Take heed to his conclusion after sampling the world's tempting fare. "Meaningless! Meaningless! . . . Everything is meaningless!" (Eccles. 12:8). When he summarized his search for the "good life," here is what he said, "Now all has been heard; here is the conclusion of the matter: Fear God and keep his commandments, for this is the whole duty of man" (Eccles. 12:13). Those are the words of one who has become a nonconformist, one disgruntled by the world's cotton candy and hungry for something of substance.

Jesus, too, warned His followers about the world's false promises. In the Sermon on the Mount, He spoke of the broad way that leads to destruction. He encouraged His people to walk a narrow way that leads to life, and we should perk our ears to the fact that He said there would be few who would find that way.

Before He died, Jesus left His disciples an alluring legacy: "Peace I leave with you; my peace I give you" (John 14:27a). He hurriedly added, "I do not give you [peace] as

26

the world gives" (John 14:27b). He was promising a peace that those on the popular road knew nothing about. Throughout His teaching, Christ outlined a way of life foreign to the ways of first-century Palestine—foreign especially to the ways of the religious elite. His message continually called people to walk a risky, different road.

Jesus' life preached nonconformity even more eloquently than His words. He was different—viewed as an eccentric, a heretic, because He refused to join the club of the religious leaders of Judaism. Throughout His life, temptations were dangled before Him, encouraging compromise and conformity at every turn. Nonetheless, He turned from every one of them, refusing to listen to the siren call of the world.

When Jesus began His public ministry, He wrestled in the wilderness with the enticements of the Tempter.

"Be a pragmatist," Jesus heard a voice say, "and turn stones into bread." (Everyone, you see, loves a man who can dole out free bread.)

"Be a negotiator, join forces with me," He heard again. "Together we can rule the world." (Wheeler-dealers, of course, get ahead in life.)

"Be sensational," He heard finally, "and *wow* the crowd by leaping from the pinnacle of the temple." (Sensationalism gets attention quickly.)

That whole temptation experience revolved around conformity. Jesus was grappling with fundamental questions about His life and ministry. Would He "go along" to "get along"? Would He play to the crowd? At the beginning of His ministry, the temptations foreshadowed the coming dilemma to be faced in the Garden of Gethsemane: conformity or the cross?

The Apostle Paul also advocated nonconformity as the way to life. "Do not conform any longer to the pattern of this world," he wrote pointedly to the Romans, "but be transformed by the renewing of your mind . . ." (Rom. 12:2). In nearly all of his letters, he preached a way of living

27

contrary to the accepted standards.

And, like Christ, Paul demonstrated what he believed. He turned his back on the approval of the world to stand before a different judge. To the Corinthians he wrote, "I care very little if I am judged by you or by any human court; indeed, I do not even judge myself . . . It is the Lord who judges me" (1 Cor. 4:3–4). Once a rising star in Judaism and well on the road to ecclesiastical success, Paul renounced his old self to live before a crowd of One. The world called him a fool, but his "foolishness" gained for Paul something that had eluded the world for a long time— inner peace. For Paul "learned to be content whatever the circumstances" (Phil. 4:11). And it was Paul, the eccentric fool, who enjoined his friends to claim "the peace of God, which transcends all understanding" (Phil. 4:7). The world could call Paul "crazy"—and it did—but he had a joy that accrues only to those on the narrow road.

The Preacher in Ecclesiastes, Jesus, and Paul all sang and lived the same melody: The crowd is untruth. Only people who hear a tune different than the world's and are willing to walk solitary paths will ever find peace.

Wearing the King's Armor

Easier said than done, however. In the world in which we find ourselves, there are deals to be struck, bills to be paid, jobs to be done and expectations to be met. Like young David standing before Goliath, we strap on the king's armor and move out into the fray. And our advisers keep insisting that the armor *is* essential. "You're expected to do this. This is the way to make it in the world." How were we to know that a slingshot and five smooth stones would be sufficient?

Jess Lair learned the hard way about the folly of heeding "everyone's" advice. In his book, *I Ain't Much, Baby— But I'm All I've Got,* he describes the misery he experienced wearing the king's armor:

The ideas in this book reflect a search that I began when I was thirty-five years old. I had an advertising agency in Minneapolis. I also did some marketing consultant work; I told businessmen how to make out plans for their business, and in some cases, executives how to plan their lives. And I had the world's greatest plan for my own life. I was going to work ten to fifteen more years at a business I hated and detested. But I was going to work a lot harder and faster so I could make a lot of money and I could retire. I had that plan all written up and one day at lunch I showed it to my financial consultant and adviser.

He looked at that plan and made some suggestions on it, but I felt funny about the whole thing. And on the way back to the office, all of a sudden I had this very strange feeling. I think what happened was my heart said to my head, "Now, look, if you are crazy enough to throw your whole life down a rat hole, chasing something that you don't believe in, that's fine. You can throw your whole life away for money and material gain. But this Norwegian heart, it ain't going to go along with you."

I had a heart attack on the way up the elevator. I staggered to my office and slumped forward on my desk until the worst of the pain went away. I got hold of a doctor across the street and foolishly told him I felt well enough to walk over.

So I walked over. He laid me out flat on an examining table and found I was right in the middle of a heart attack. He called an ambulance, they put me on a stretcher and hauled me to the hospital.

As I lay there in that hospital bed, I thought to myself, "Boy, somehow you've gone a long, long way down the wrong path through a whole, long series of rotten sick, destructive choices. You've gone into things that you've got no sense being in. There is almost nothing left in your life of what you really are." And the resolution that I made, in one of those lucid moments when one is intensely calm, was *from this time on I am never again going to do what I don't deeply believe in.* And that decision, made under that kind of pressure, has stuck with me pretty much ever since.

Not everyone has a heart attack from trying to bear the weight of the king's armor. But everyone who lives by some artificially drawn up, mass-produced plan of life suffers. If we spend our lives doing things we don't really believe in, something has to give. In Jess Lair's case, it was a heart. But sometimes it's a marriage, or a relationship with a child, or intimacy with God, or inner peace. Though it looks beneficial and everyone else is wearing it, the king's armor exacts an awful toll.

Listening to Our Lives

As I suggested at the end of the last chapter, we foster peace by listening to our lives—and to God's still, small voice deep within us.

If God has spoken to me at all—and I believe He has—this is how He has done it. He has tapped out His will for me in what Frederick Buechner calls "the alphabet of grace":

> You wake up out of the huge crevices of the night and your dreaming. You get out of bed, wash and dress, eat breakfast, say goodbye and go away never maybe to return for all you know, to work, talk, lust, pray, dawdle and do, and at the end of the day, if your luck holds, you come home again, home again. Then night again. Bed. The little death of sleep, sleep of death. Morning, afternoon, evening—the hours of the day, of any day, or your day and my day. The alphabet of grace. If there is a God who speaks anywhere, surely he speaks here: through waking up and working, through going away and coming back again, through people you read and books you meet, through falling asleep in the dark.

I have often wished that God would thunder edicts from heaven or, in some other way, directly guide my destiny. I have prayed for signs and put out fleeces. But God has always spoken most eloquently to me through that quiet voice, that voice that can easily be ignored. The truth is, if we miss that quiet voice, we miss God.

Stress is a warning signal that tells you and me something important about our lives. So does depression, gladness, apathy, habits, sleeping and eating patterns, illnesses. Those are all signals telling us who we are, what we love and what we hate, how we ought to be spending our days. If we ignore those signals—and most of us do—we will miss out on God's joy and peace. We will doctor sick people when we ought to be plowing fields, make investments when we ought to be making love, climb corporate ladders when we ought to be teaching third-graders, plod around in bulky armor when we should be dashing through meadows with slingshots. We will miss life as it flies by.

What About "The Will of God"?

I have done a lot of struggling with the concept of the will of God. I have read about it, pondered it, preached it and tried ceaselessly to find it for myself. My conclusion after the wrestling match? Much of our thinking about God's will is false.

In my religious training, the will of God was presented as a checklist of things to be accomplished—be nice to people, read the Bible, go to church, be honest, tithe, and other righteous deeds. I have no doubt that God wills us to do those things. They must be part of His will for us. But living by the divine checklist is not all there is to God's will. The checklist concept of the will of God is not complete, first, because it is too "external." That is, it has little to do with that inner sensor God has given us—His still, small voice. The checklist has everything to do with brittle commandments and nothing to do with a father's voice that warms and thrills. Second, it's too "general." It lumps everybody into one bundle, the human race, and implies that God's will is that we all live just alike. There is no room in the checklist concept for particularity.

That is why I prefer Robert Capon's definition, in *Hunt-*

31

ing the Divine Fox: "The will of God is not a list of stops for us to make to pick up mouthwash, razor blades and a pound of chopped chuck on the way home. It is his longing that we will take the risk of being nothing but ourselves, desperately in love."

Have you ever thought of God's will like that? He is longing for us to take the risk of being nothing but ourselves, desperately in love. That definition, for me, tingles with life and good news! God wants me to tune in and listen to Him, to be the special creation He handcrafted me to be. He longs for me to be myself—in love with Him, with people and with life.

For Richer or Poorer

A surprise awaits those who will take the risk of being nothing but themselves. In daring to be different, we magnetize our lives and begin to attract people, ideas, and activities that further enrich life and deepen its joy. A positive cycle is set in motion. We listen to God, take a few faltering steps, find affirmation and a few kindred spirits and increase our joy. We decide we like the direction we're headed, listen a little more, and take a few more steps toward authenticity. We're on a roll, moving in the direction of God's will, and that is life's most fulfilling journey.

Often we say that living for God is hard. We think that doing life God's way is a tough, uphill struggle. Actually, just the reverse is true. God's will defines the natural flow our lives are supposed to take, the path our inner sensor is nudging us toward. Going that way may set us at odds with the masses, but it *will* lead to His peace.

The people who find life a tough, uphill struggle are those deaf to who they are supposed to be, those too busy to hear a still, small voice. They become alienated from themselves and those who would love them in their peculiarity. They work at the wrong jobs, invest their time in the wrong activities and generally make a mess of their lives. Talk about stress! Their whole existence is at odds with God's will, and they experience nothing but constant frustration. This cycle of alienation will continue until something causes the person to probe his misery and make some radical changes. When he finally starts listening to God and obeying His voice, then the positive cycle of harmony will begin to affect every area of his life.

After he told the parable of the talents, Jesus said, "For everyone who has will be given more, and he will have an abundance. Whoever does not have, even what he has will be taken from him" (Matt. 25:29). That sounds strange. In effect, the rich will get richer and the poor will get poorer. But that is a law of life, imprinted indelibly in the human spirit.

Those who have much—in terms of faith, hope, love, and other virtues—set in motion that positive cycle of harmony. They move from joy to deeper joy, peace to greater peace. They have learned how to get rich and so get richer. On the other hand, those who have little, in terms of the necessary virtues, perpetuate the alienation cycle and move from misery to more misery, stress to more stress. They are poor and, unless they change, are destined to become even poorer.

All of us are caught in one of those two cycles. We're headed either *for* the abundant life or *away* from it.

Helen and Randy are caught in the negative cycle. So are thousands of their comrades in the modern church. Hearing sermons, bear in mind, is not the same as hearing God. Going to church, remember, doesn't guarantee faithfulness to inner promptings. It is possible to be a model of piety and the pillar of the church and still be light years away from the will of God.

Signing Up for the Trip

What should we do if we see we are drifting away from the abundant life? The beginning point is your willingness

33

to be a nonconformist. Paul's "do not conform . . . but be transformed" plea provides the philosophical, theological foundation we need to start our journey to peace. Until we will risk being different, until we are fed up with the popular plan for success, we are not ready for the trip. We cannot go with half-hearted commitment. We cannot navigate the trail with one eye cocked to the crowd.

The traveler on this expedition must meet only two qualifications: (1) He or she must be somewhat disillusioned with life as it is, and (2) he or she must take a pledge to be a "nonconformist," in the sense we've just described. If you qualify, read on.

For Reflection and Discussion

1. Do you believe that the popular, well-traveled road to success is a dead end? If so, how did you come to that conclusion?

2. Read two chapters from the book of Ecclesiastes each night this week and notice how contemporary the preacher's search for the "good life" seems. Do you agree with the Preacher's conclusion at the end of his book?

3. Have you ever personally tried to "wear the king's armor"? To be something you aren't?

4. Do you believe that "everyone who lives by some artificially drawn up, mass-produced plan of life suffers?" Are you suffering now because of your attempt to conform?

5. How long has it been since you listened to God's still small voice and took a risk because of an inner prompting?

6. Have you felt depressed lately? Had trouble sleeping? Felt bored or listless? Been sick more than usual? Had conflict in some of your relationships? Felt restless or anxious? What are these things trying to tell you?

7. What do you think of the idea of the will of God as "taking the risk of being nothing but ourselves, desperately in love"?

8. In terms of joy, are you growing richer or poorer? Are you moving toward the abundant life or away from it?

If God is for us, who can be against us?

Romans 8:31

"Perhaps the devil's actual work is to strike such terror into human souls that they perceive God as a tyrant father who exacts work from his children by caning and cudgeling them."

Edna Hong, *The Downward Ascent*

3

THE GOD OF WORRY

T spent most of my childhood terrified of Doyle Jennings, who was a couple of years older than I and recognized locally as the neighborhood bully. The ultimate fear among my group of friends was to bump into Doyle in one of his bad moods. Rumor had it that Doyle regularly pummeled people just for the fun of it. Naturally, we avoided as much as possible riding our bicycles by his house, which sat sullenly on the corner by the elementary school.

The irony is that Doyle Jennings never pummeled any of us. We had heard of his exploits from classmates but, as far as I remember, none of us ever suffered his wrath personally. In fact, the few times I couldn't avoid Doyle, he was reasonably pleasant and cordial. It is distinctly possible that he was not nearly the villain we imagined him to be. If he, by some small chance, reads this book, he will probably be amazed to learn that he struck such terror in our hearts.

Repeating the Original Sin

It seems to me that God has also picked up an undeserved bad reputation. Listen to people who spew theology and you will notice it. To hear people tell it—even church people who have been in Sunday school all their lives—God is a Stern Bookkeeper, a Vengeful Judge, a Heavy-handed Moralist, a Holy Warrior. Of course, these people will not use such terms to describe the deity. They will actually speak of Him as love and call him Father. But peel away the veneer, look beneath the pious words, and you will hear the truth: People generally feel about God the way I felt about Doyle Jennings. Religious rhetoric notwithstanding, the average person has a wrong concept of God.

I believe it is this wrong concept of God that adds to the stress level in the lives of many believers. Until we understand and undo our wrong thinking, it may be that our "Christianity" is actually killing us, rather than bringing us abundant life.

We shouldn't be shocked by that notion. The oldest trick on record was when the Tempter seduced Adam and Eve into thinking that God was against them. Satan convinced them that God was the enemy, withholding both fruit and wisdom from them. They believed the lie, committed the original sin, and stumbled out of the Garden of Eden.

It's incredible, isn't it, that the lie persists after all these years, and that modern men still believe it? Surely the absurdity of that lie would have been made plain to us by now. But it hasn't. I listen to countless men, women and teenagers, in the privacy of my office, who still believe the lie. Their God is stern, rigid, unforgiving. They call Him "righteous" and "holy," but what that really translates into is "unapproachable."

The Tempter is still spinning the deception, and gullible men and women are still seeing God as the Cosmic Bully.

But What About. . . ?

I know, I know. Your mind is racing back to all of those Old Testament passages that seem to say that God is, indeed, the Cosmic Bully. You remember disobedient people being turned into pillars of salt, and enemy tribes being slaughtered at Yahweh's command. You recall harsh Levitical laws and fierce warnings of doom from God's prophets. You're wondering how I can so blithely tiptoe around those passages and believe in a God of unparalleled, undiluted love.

My response is that I believe those Old Testament passages are not the *final* revelation of who God is. If we want to know about the character of God, we have to gaze long and hard at Jesus of Nazareth, not only at the wrathful God of Obadiah and Zechariah. As the writer of Hebrews puts it:

> In the past, God spoke to our forefathers through the prophets at many times and various ways, but in these last days he has spoken to us by his Son, whom he appointed heir of all things, and through whom he made the universe. The Son is the radiance of God's glory and the exact representation of his being (Heb. 1:1–3).

I can tell you that God is 100 percent pure love because I have looked at, and listened to, Jesus. I have heard Him tell of a prodigal son who was given a party, or lavish wages given to undeserving laborers, of crooked but penitent tax collectors warmly welcomed into God's kingdom. And of all the terms Jesus could have picked to define God, the one He chose was Father. Father—not Judge, or Most High Potentate, or Nebulous, Unknowable One. Father—better yet, Daddy. Remember how Jesus answered Mary on resurrection morning: "I am returning to my Father and your Father . . ." (John 20:17). Jesus tells me volumes about the character of God.

And I have looked upon the cross. I have stood on Golgotha and reflected on how God-in-the-flesh died between two thieves to show, once and for all, the extent of His love. John Killinger, in one of his sermons, has said that Jesus was God's way of getting rid of a bad reputation, and nowhere is that more evident than at the cross. "But God demonstrates his own love for us in this: While we were still sinners, Christ died for us" (Rom. 5:8).

What that death so plainly says is that God loves us. After all of the old laws and strange customs and prophetic harangues, God put an end to the debate about His character by dying for the world. "Greater love has no one than this, that one lay down his life for his friends" (John 15:13). How long will it take us to catch on? Why are we so slow to perceive the love of God? How could He have conveyed it to us more persuasively? Surely the cross was the most eloquent love letter in the history of the universe—and still we keep looking over our shoulder to see what God thinks of us.

My forebear, Jonathan Edwards, is remembered for his famous sermon called "Sinners in the Hands of an Angry God." At the risk of sounding haughty, I must disagree with the picture my celebrated kinsman paints of the nature of God. If we are sinners in the hands of an angry God, whose wrath burns and burns, what hope is left for us? Surely we are doomed despite all of our efforts to be holy and righteous and presentable to God. What could possibly alter such anger?

I believe we are sinners in the hands of a *loving* God. The cross demonstrates unmistakably that God has seen our plight and raced to the rescue. Just because the prison door is open, however, doesn't mean we have to walk through it. Certainly, we can reject our freedom, and keep scratching to earn God's favor. But the truth is: "Christ died for sins once for all, the righteous for the unrighteous, to bring you to God" (1 Pet. 3:18).

God *has* loved us. Jesus *has* died for us. We are free to go.

Climbing the Motivation Ladder

I don't think I am oversimplifying to suggest that all of us relate to God in one of three ways. In terms of our personal motivation to live for God, we all fall into one of three groups.

First, there are those who have no motivation to live for God at all. They are on the bottom rung of the motivation ladder. For whatever reason, they seem oblivious to the spiritual dimension of life. They are not bad people, but there seems to be no hunger for God evidenced in their lives. They may be intelligent, hold high-paying jobs, raise normal kids and have impeccable morals. But they are deaf to God and ignorant of the things of the Spirit.

In His parable of the sower, Jesus tells about some people whose lives are like the soil by the wayside. When the seed, the word of God, falls upon them, it never takes root. The soil is so packed, so impenetrable, the seed can't even begin to grow. Sadly, some people are like the soil by the wayside and never get motivated to "bring forth fruit."

Then there are those who are motivated by fear. This is a higher level of motivation than none at all, and many fine folks live their whole lives on this second rung of the ladder. But I am personally convinced that God wants us to climb above this level.

When I was in the fifth grade, I had a teacher who made going to school a nightmare. She was tall and fearsome, and we all trembled in her presence. She regularly reduced some of us to tears with her stern rebukes. You can be sure we did our homework for her class and tried our best never even to whisper. In retrospect, I can see that it was better to learn out of fear than not to learn at all. But, learning or no learning, we were miserable in that woman's class, and I can relive my dread to this day.

Like me in the fifth grade, there are Christians who are miserable and uptight in their relationship to God. There's no joy in a relationship based on fear, and if, as the Bible asserts over and over again, God wants us to know joy, He must have something else in mind for us.

Which brings us to the highest rung on the motivation ladder: We are motivated by love. We taste the delicious love of God and spend the rest of our days celebrating it. Our motto becomes:

> There is no fear in love. But perfect love drives out
> fear, because fear has to do with punishment. The man

41

who fears is not made perfect in love. We love because
he first loved us (1 John 4:18–19).

I had another teacher in my younger days, too, who
also left an indelible mark on me. She was my fourth grade
teacher, and I loved her like a mother.

Out of all the kids in the class, she seemed to like me
best. She took me to football games on Saturday after-
noons. She asked me to run errands and do favors for her.
She taught me French and manners before school. It was
obvious that I was her "pet," and I reveled in her love. You
can be sure that I never missed a homework assignment in
her class or spoke without raising my hand. I knew I was
her favorite student, and I couldn't bear to disappoint her.
To this day, I can still relive the joy of going to school in
the fourth grade, the wonder of learning new truths, and
the surprise of being the apple of someone's eye.

Can you appreciate the difference in what I experienced those two years in elementary school? I learned both
years. But one year was miserable because of fear; the
other delightful because of love. That's the way it is in our
Christian experience. We can be miserable, uptight Christians because of fear—or we can be relaxed, joyful Christians because we know we are the apple of Someone's eye.

This third level of motivation is where God wants us to
dwell. He wants us to know Him as "Father." He wants us
to look again and again at the cross and drink in the extent
of His love for us. And He wants us to live secure and
restful lives in relationship to Him.

A Saccharine Deity?

Someone may protest, "Your God is just the Sweet Old
Man in the Sky. A soft, toothless Sugar Daddy. I can't be-
lieve in that kind of God. Give me a God who's tough, a
God with backbone."

God *is* tough enough to set us free and let us ruin our
lives if we choose to do so. He is tough enough to let us

doubt His love and live as if the cross never happened. He is tough enough to watch in agony as we ruin His proposed paradise. He is tough enough, in other words, to grant us freedom to believe or not believe, freedom to become or not become.

Anyone with children knows how much backbone it takes to set those children free, and the heavenly Father has courage enough—a love tough enough—to grant us unlimited liberty. Karl Olsson, in *Come to the Party,* says:

> The God who has established my identity and the cosmos it occupies has left me free to go in any direction. The song, "I want to be me, I want to be free" is, as far as it goes, the situation into which we have been created. The bondages that have been imposed on my me-ness or freeness are not of God's making. They have been forged by people and by circumstances and most probably by myself.

God is even tough enough, mind you, to go with us when freedom pushes us into our personal hells. At the cross God showed His operative mode: He suffers *with* the world to redeem it. When we come to the end of ourselves, when the grief is too much or the pressure too great, we discover, to our amazement, that:

> If I make my bed in the depths, you are there (Ps. 139:8).

God is tough enough to stay with us when everyone else has deserted us and headed for cooler places.

Lewis Smedes found out about God's tough love and described it like this in his book, *How Can It Be All Right When Everything's All Wrong?*:

> It happened to me on a sunny September Wednesday; I fell into my mini-hell and landed in the hands of the living God. I cannot provide the details of the fall; twenty-five years of thinking and teaching about God's ways leave me with no verbal tools to do more than say how it felt to me. My savvy friends who know all about psychology will tell you I had an acute anxiety attack.

43

Maybe they are right. I can only tell you that what I experienced was the saving presence of a loving God who put his hands under me when I was dangling, dry, hung out in nothingness where no human hand was able to reach out and hold me up. . . .

I discovered, all by myself, in touch only with my final outpost of feeling, that I could be left, deserted, alone, all my scaffolds knocked down, all the stanchions beneath me pulled away, my buttresses fallen, I could be stripped of human hands, and I could survive. In my deepest heart, I survived, stood up, stayed whole, held by nothing at all except the grace of God.

If God Is for Us. . .

Just *suppose* that the God of the universe wants us to know joy. Suppose that the One who sprinkled the galaxies into the heavens knows us intimately and wants to work in our behalf. Wouldn't that be incredible? Wouldn't we approach every day with gratitude and expectancy? Wouldn't our attitude be transformed?

According to the New Testament, that is exactly our situation! God wills our joy. He knows the number of hairs on our head and the latest thought that sprinted through our brain, and He wants to set us free to live abundantly. He is our "Abba Father," and He is *for* us. If we ever question that, all we have to do is reread the love letter he penned at Calvary.

One day the Apostle Paul sat scrunched in a prison cell and started to sing at the top of his lungs: "If God is for us, who can be against us?"

Think about that for a moment. If it is true that God is for us, that He is on our side working for our good, what can ultimately defeat us?

If God is for us, can any earthly setback permanently douse our joy?

If God is for us, can't we know we will eventually triumph over the depression, the divorce, the death of our loved one?

If God is for us, isn't most of our worry a life-draining lack of faith?

If God is for us, isn't even the fear of death diminished—or maybe removed?

If God is for us, isn't the only thing that can destroy our peace the *refusal to believe* that He is for us?

Choose Your Theology

Most of us have a difficult time believing that God is for us. Or we believe it with our head but not with our heart. When we find ourselves moving away from the abundant life, it is high time to look again at our theology to see if a faulty view of God is creating some of our misery.

What we think and feel about God is crucial to our lives. All of us have some concept of God, a theology, whether healthy or unhealthy. Often we try to plead ignorance about theology because we're not seminary trained or because we have a hard time understanding the Bible. Such avoidance of spiritual realities only places us in jeopardy, though. An ostrich with its head in the sand, contrary to what it thinks, is not safe.

Annie Dillard's question, in *Teaching a Stone to Talk*, is worth pondering:

> Why do we people in churches seem like cheerful, brainless tourists on a packaged tour of the Absolute?
>
> The tourists have coffee and doughnuts on Deck C. Presumably someone is minding the ship, avoiding icebergs and shoals, fueling the engines, watching the radar screen, noting weather reports radioed in from shore. No one would dream of asking the tourists to do these things. Alas, among the tourists on Deck C, drinking coffee and eating doughnuts, we find the captain, and all the ship's officers, and all the ship's crew. The officers chat; they swear; they wink a bit at slightly raw jokes, just like regular people. The crew members have funny accents. The wind seems to be picking up.

The wind *is* picking up, and we'd all better have some

45

idea of how to navigate our theological ship. We can't rely on the preacher or the Sunday-school teacher to get us home. We have to forge our own theology. We have to have a personal relationship with God. We have to forego the coffee and doughnuts and tend to more significant matters. If we don't, the icebergs will surely prevail.

My only advice to all of us amateur theologians is to remember to keep our eyes resolutely fixed on Jesus and His cross. That, it seems to me, is the main attraction of Christianity. All of the other biblical material is a sideshow to the one grand event in the center ring: God-Man dying for our sins. It is possible to become so enamored with sideshows that we lose sight of the one event that ought to shape our theology, and our lives, more than any other: Jesus has died to set us free. Once we get that linchpin firmly in place, we're well on the way to a theology that leads to peace and joy. The more we study the cross, the more implications we will see that lead to abundant living.

The other night at the pizza place the kids' placemats each had a picture of a clown. The instructions said to find eight things wrong with the picture. At first glance, it looked like an ordinary clown. But closer inspection revealed otherwise: The paint around one eye was different than the paint around the other, one ear was smaller than the other, one dot on the costume was unpainted, and so forth. Careful scrutiny uncovered more than we saw in our initial glance.

That's the way it is with Jesus and His cross. At first glance, you think you see a Jewish peasant dying an ordinary death between two thieves. Or, if you've been to church all your life, you see something you've seen so often you don't notice anything special about it at all. But if you look closely and study it with new eyes, you begin to notice things in the picture you never suspected were there: hope, peace, joy, an end to any need to try to impress God, a life of gratitude.

If you gaze long enough at the cross, you will find that

your uptight, downcast attitude will be transformed into the laughter of the free.

Laughing With Lazarus

Eugene O'Neill's play *Laughing with Lazarus* begins with Jesus' raising of Lazarus from the dead and deals with the change this miracle makes in Lazarus' life. After he has been raised, Lazarus becomes fearless. Try as they might, the Jewish leaders cannot stifle his gladness. Laughter is his trademark, and everywhere he goes people are warmed and enlivened by his presence. Because he has learned that even the Final Enemy cannot defeat him, Lazarus is eternally infected with joy. It's a scenario we uptight Christians would do well to consider.

Sheer fiction you say? A figment of the playwright's imagination? Not really—for we are like Lazarus! We are the people who have been raised to walk in newness of life. We are the ones who insist that the hope of the resurrection affects us profoundly the moment we choose Jesus. Every last one of us who claims to be a Christian has as an inheritance the same joy Lazarus experienced after his miracle at Bethany. The same fearlessness. The same contagious freedom.

The only bucket of water hanging over the fire is our unbelief. At heart, you see, we are unbelievers. We refuse to accept all of the incredible implications of Calvary. We believe the lie that God is not for us. Though the prison door stands wide open, we huddle in self-imposed chains and refuse to claim our liberty. Unlike Lazarus, we refuse to leave the tomb. We cannot get our heart to believe that laughter is our birthright.

But, thank God, it is never too late! The door stands eternally open. And our joy and peace are the surest indicators we have walked through it.

So, if you want to know just how Christian you really are, don't listen to your creeds or your prayers. They come from your head and reflect your mind. Listen, instead, to your laughter. It comes from your soul and reflects your heart. Your laughter will tell you unfailingly of your faith in God.

A "Batting Stance" that Works

Any fourth-rate ballplayer can tell you the proper technique for hitting the ball—get the bat off your shoulder, keep your head down, step into the ball, swing level. But the real payoff is in the box score: How many hits did the batter actually get? Sound *technique* means nothing unless the hitter gets consistent wood on the ball.

That's the way it is with our theology. All of our venerable doctrines are useless unless they accomplish something tangible. And what, in this analogy, is a base hit for the Christian? The Apostle Paul says, "The fruit of the Spirit is love, joy, peace, patience, kindness, goodness, faithfulness, gentleness, and self-control" (Gal. 5:22–23).

Even if our doctrines are impeccable, they profit us little if we cannot translate them into love, joy, peace, patience, kindness, goodness, faithfulness, gentleness, and self-control. The truest test of our faith is not what we believe, but what we *do* with our beliefs. Regardless of our orthodoxy, if we cannot laugh, if we cannot love, if we have no peace, if no fruit ever blooms, we are nowhere near the kingdom of God.

All of us who are uptight Christians, then, will probably have to concede that our test of orthodoxy has been askew. We have been so enamored with batting stances that we have failed to check our box score for base hits. If our view of God is contributing to our uptightness, our joylessness, something is sorely amiss. *God is for us.* Why don't we act like it?

Any sandlot ballplayer could at least tell us this much: When you're in a slump and striking out consistently, it may be time to try another stance.

For Reflection and Discussion

1. Do you think it is true that the "average person has a wrong concept of God"?

2. Do you agree that "Jesus was God's way of getting rid of a bad reputation"? Why or why not?

3. Does the concept of God sketched in this chapter seem too forebearing to you? With what, in particular, do you agree or disagree?

4. Have you ever fallen into your own mini-hell? Did you sense the presence of God there?

5. If you truly believed God wanted you to experience unrestrained joy, what would it do to your life? What changes would you have to make?

6. Where are you now on "the motivation ladder"?

7. How much of your theology is your own, and how much of it have you accepted without really thinking about it?

8. What change do you need to make in your "batting stance"?

9. Rate yourself on a scale of 1–10:

   _____ Love   _____ Patience   _____ Faithfulness
   _____ Joy   _____ Kindness   _____ Gentleness
   _____ Peace   _____ Goodness   _____ Self-control

10. How much of your stress comes from a faulty view of God?

So God created man in his own image, in the image of God he created them; male and female he created them.

Genesis 1:27

"For a man or woman to take anything, to take any raw material like lumber or words, and shape these formless materials into a pattern that bears the stamp of his or her brain or hand, is the most satisfying thing to do in the whole world. It's why I object to cake mixes."

Andy Rooney, "The Ultimate Vacation" in the *Houston Chronicle*

4

DAMMING THE RIVER

I recently clipped from the Houston *Post* an article about a couple who have an intriguing enterprise in their home. Dick Hill whittles decoys and fashions lifelike sculptures of ducks from blocks of wood. Cissie, his wife, paints the decoys and pencils in the feathers. Together, they produce twenty-five to thirty birds a month, which earns them a surprisingly handsome living.

But it's not the money that delights them most. They get their greatest joy from making decoys that are works of art. "It's tiring and tedious, but you get to make something new," Dick says. "The only reason I like carving is it's open-ended. No matter how good I get, I can never get where I want to be. There are always new horizons. That means a lot to me."

"A hundred years from now," Cissie adds, "our work will still be here. It'll be here when we're not." And the Hills' creative endeavors have provided them another precious commodity. "This has given us so much freedom," Cissie says. "We can live where we want to live. We can work as we want. We don't have to take orders from anybody."

Created to Create

I cut that article from the paper not because I'm planning a new career in decoy-carving, but because I'm fascinated by creativity. I clip articles about writers, poets, innovative preachers and the creative process itself. When I flip through those articles again, my joy level inevitably rises. I find myself more motivated to get my own creative juices flowing. Those articles remind me that I too was created to create.

The writer of Genesis tells us that God created man in His own image. He does not specify, however, what "in His own image" means. It could mean that, like God, man was made to give and receive love. Or it could mean that man has a conscience, a God-implanted sense of "oughtness." Or it could mean that man was made to rule, to have dominion over the rest of creation. Take your pick—"in His own image" could imply any or all of those things.

But it could also mean that God the Creator fashioned man to be creator also. For us to be created in God's image could denote our special calling to join Him in the act of creation. Because we were built from a divine pattern, we have been given special powers to bring new things into existence—duck decoys, ceramic pots, patchwork quilts, songs, poems, novels, apple pies or whatever else it gives us delight to make. To repress that creative impulse may well be a sinful repudiation of the divine intent.

Sometimes we fall prey to the mistaken notion that only certain people are creative. We dub poets and painters "creative"; accountants and garbage collectors are "uncreative." It is certainly true that some people exhibit their creativity more than others and respond to the creative impulse more faithfully, but all people have the God-given capacity to create.

Bronowski, in *A Sense of the Future*, writes, "To my mind, it is a mistake to think of creative activity as something unusual. I hold that the creative activity is normal to all living things. Creation is the finding of order in what was disorderly, and this is a characteristic of human activity."

And Nicolas Berdyaev reminds us, in *The Destiny of Man*, "God created man in his own image and likeness, i.e., made him a creator too, calling him to free spontaneous activity and not to formal obedience to his power. Free creativeness is the creature's answer to the great call of its Creator. Man's creative work is the fulfillment of the Creator's secret will." In truth, *all* of us were created to create, and if we neglect our creativity we are something less than God intended.

I think we all receive the summons: "You are hereby invited to build a table, letter a sign, compose a song, bake a loaf of bread, sew a dress." And then we either answer the summons positively or negatively. We either roll up our sleeves and start creating, or we keep our hands in our pockets and walk away from the invitation. In *The Irrational Season*, Madeleine L'Engle observes:

> I am convinced that each work of art, be it a great work of genius or something very small, has its own life, and it will come to the artist, the composer or the writer or the painter, and say, "Here I am: compose me; or write me; or paint me"; and the job of the artist is to serve the work. I have never served a work as I would like to, but I do try, with each book, to serve to the best of my ability, and this attempt at serving is the greatest privilege and the greatest joy I know.

We either "serve the work" or we don't.

The Pain of Creating

So why don't we create? Why don't we eagerly answer the summons in the affirmative? Why don't we do a better job of "serving the work"—be it bread or a book?

Well, for one reason, creating something involves pain. It costs to create. The bread or the book often demands more from us than we are willing to give.

Let me deal specifically with the one creative endeavor with which I am most familiar—writing. Writing is a sweet agony. There is nothing that gives me greater pleasure than to concoct well-crafted sentences, or to string those sentences into a tight paragraph, or to bundle those paragraphs into a book that reads easy and right. For me, there is no joy like the one that comes from writing something well.

And yet, I will do almost anything to keep from writing because writing is such hard work. Writing beckons, and I keep denying the summons. I have too much "to do": too many people to see, sermons to prepare, administrative duties to perform. And what if no publisher wants my stuff? Why should I spend hours and days and months on a book that may prove to be a colossal exercise in futility?

Finally, though, I somehow bite the bullet.

Yet as I write, I find a swarm of reasons to escape the rigors of writing. I need a drink, so I put the pen down and venture to the water fountain down the hall. Or I think of someone I need to call. Or I pick up a book I've been meaning to read for a long time. Or I start shuffling the mess on my desk into neat piles.

Someone once said, "Most young men have no desire to write. They prefer to have written." I know exactly what that means. There is no greater thrill, to me, than seeing my name on a book jacket. There is also no greater pain than having to glue my breeches to a chair and create that book.

I assume that what is true of writing is also true of other creative endeavors as well. I'm sure there are some days when the Hills would just as soon not carve their decoys, the painter would rather not paint, and the photographer would prefer not to take pictures. Nobody ever said creating was easy. God himself had to take a break after His grand act of creation was finished!

Thomas Edison once said that genius is one percent inspiration and ninety-nine percent perspiration. The same can be said for creativity. And we don't create as much or as well as we should because we're not too fond of perspiration. The creative impulse is quickly choked by our laziness.

But few things bring joy like the act of creating. Andy Rooney is right: When we have fashioned something that bears the stamp of our own brain or hand, we have done the most satisfying thing in the whole world. And wouldn't it be tragic if we let our laziness snuff out one of our greatest sources of joy?

Caring Enough to Create

There may be a second, even more indicting, reason why we don't use our creative powers: We may not *care* enough. Laziness is bad; not caring is even worse. But creativity is always connected to caring about things, and if we don't care we simply won't create.

Let me illustrate by returning to the written word. There is no doubt that I write because I care so much about books. My writing is anchored to my love for the printed page.

Years ago I admitted that I am an advanced "bookaholic." I have lived with severe "bibliomania" for a long time and suspect it may be a lifetime affliction. I have even now just returned from a trip to the shopping mall where I purchased two more books for my collection—a biography of E. B. White and a book of essays about baseball. I will read them and then proudly place them on the shelves with hundreds of other books. I don't know where this infatuation with books came from; I only know it got mysteriously woven into my heart. "Bookaholics" like myself don't just read books. We caress them, smell them, feel the texture of the pages, memorize the author's names, and take great pleasure in lining the walls with them. A "book-aholic" is certain of at least one thing: heaven will undoubtedly have a bookstore.

My love of books is, I think, the source of my desire to write them. The caring precedes and produces the creating. And I'm sure this is true of all creative works. They sprout from the soil of someone's delight. Only those who care, who find a particular facet of life fascinating, will ever create. When the baker loses his love for baking, the apple pies will lose their flavor. When the artist loses her enchantment with color and texture, her paintings will no longer inspire. When the preacher forgets the wonder of the gospel, his sermons will become drudgery for everyone, including himself. A creation detached from delight gives little joy to anyone.

Caring is actually the glue that holds culture together. When people stop caring, society starts to unravel. Bread goes unbaked, poems unwritten, and children undisciplined. Caring, and the creating it motivates, makes the city of man a community:

> Culture can come only from caring enough about things to want them really to be themselves—to want the poem to scan perfectly, the song to be genuinely melodic, the basketball actually to drop through the middle of the hoop, the edge of the board to be utterly straight, the pastry to be really flaky. Few of us have very many great things to care about, but we all have plenty of small ones; and that's enough for the dance. It is precisely through the things we put on the table, and the liturgies we form around it, that the city is built; *caring* is more than half the work.

When Robert Farrar Capon penned those lines, in *Bed and Board*, he could not have been more perceptive.

Left-Brained Christians

There is a third reason we are not better creators: We live in a technological, analytical society that discourages creativity. We have all been conditioned to be uncreative.

The human brain has two hemispheres. The "left brain" breaks the mind's pictures into component parts, analyzes data, computes probabilities, and files information under headings. It likes to work quickly, efficiently and abstractly. And it's a phenomenal computer.

The "right brain" perceives the world in a different way. It *notices* things. It sees bark on trees and lines on faces. It loves to linger over details. The "right brain" enables us to hear and appreciate music, for example. It takes individual music notes and understands them to be a melody. It takes the individual words of a poem and translates them into images, visions, and goose bumps. If there is coming a day, as the prophet Joel predicts, when old men will dream dreams and young men will see visions, it will be the "right brain" that brings it to pass.

But it is the "right brain" that is jeopardized in our scientific culture. The "left brain" is exercised regularly, not only in the market place but also in the church. We Christians are experts at memorizing, dogmatizing, pigeon-holing, organizing, and programming—all "left brain" functions. We are not so adept, however, at dreaming dreams, seeing visions, appreciating fine music, or bringing new things into being.

Ever since the sixteenth century and the beginning of what we call modern science, Western culture and religion have been captivated by the abstract and analytical. For several hundred years now, the left side of the brain has been growing fat and sassy while the creative right side has atrophied and been left for dead. We can't create and dream and feel as we should, because the abstract "left brain" has bullied the "right brain" into submission.

Long before science knew anything about the brain having two hemispheres with distinct functions, Charles Darwin wrote something that may all too accurately describe our plight. Virginia Stem Owens reports in her essay, *Seeing Christianity in Red and Green as Well as Black and*

White," that, in his later years, long after his notable scientific achievements, Darwin sounded one note of regret:

> I have said that in one respect my mind has changed during the last twenty or thirty years. Up to the age of thirty, or beyond it, poetry of many kinds . . . gave me great pleasure, and even as a schoolboy I took intense delight in Shakespeare. . . . I have also said that formerly pictures gave me considerable, and music very great, delight. But now for many years I cannot endure to read a line of poetry: I have tried to read Shakespeare, and found it so intolerably dull that it nauseated me. I have also lost any taste for pictures or music. . . . I retain some taste for fine scenery, but it does not cause me the exquisite delight which it formerly did. . . . My mind seems to have become a kind of machine for grinding general laws out of large collections of facts, but why this should have caused the atrophy of that part of the brain alone, on which the higher tastes depend, I cannot conceive. . . . The loss of these tastes is a loss of happiness, and may possibly be injurious to the intellect, and more probably to the moral character, by enfeebling the emotional part of our nature.

That diagnosis has proven to be surprisingly accurate. It is probable that a part of Darwin's brain *had* atrophied through lack of use, and the same thing can happen (has happened?) to many of us.

Can we love God with our whole mind, as Jesus commands us, if we neglect the creative right hemisphere? Are we being responsible stewards if we use only half a brain? Is it even possible to experience the abundant life and know true joy if we shut down half our mind?

Feeding the Lake

The answer, obviously, is no. We must continually fight off laziness, apathy, and abstraction and use our God-given power to create. Owens also quotes author Jean Rhys, who once told an interviewer, "Listen to me. All of writing is a huge lake. There are great rivers that feed the lake, like Tolstoy and Dostoyevsky. And there are mere trickles, like Jean Rhys. All that matters is feeding the lake. I don't matter. The lake matters. You must keep feeding the lake."

That lake—the one filled with written words—is not the only lake in the world either. There are "lakes" filled with songs and strudels and sketches, and our charge is to feed those lakes with the products of our hands and hearts.

Each of us has a particular gift to offer God and our fellow human beings. Our gift may seem paltry, a mere trickle, but that is not the issue. Our calling is to sing, write, dance, design—in short, to add our tiny trickle to the ocean that is ultimately God's kingdom here on earth.

What, you may be wondering, does feeding the lake have to do with our stress? What does creativity have to do with our uptight condition? Quite a bit, actually. If it is true that God created us to create, we cannot fulfill our design if we're not creating. If we dam up that creative river, we are at odds with our purpose and doom ourselves to frustration and anxiety. Only when the dammed river finds an outlet will it ever become a gently flowing stream.

Besides, the best antidote for stress is delight, and creativity is surrounded by it. As I said earlier, creativity grows out of delight, but it also *produces* delight. The whole creative process is hemmed in by joy. When we begin to unleash our particular creative gift that God has bestowed upon us, we will begin to find a delightful fulfillment that holds our uptight misery at bay. Our frazzled nerves will be healed and we will begin to be at peace.

Let us begin, then, to create. Let us feed the lake with the treasures only our hands and hearts can fashion. Let us make our lives a special creation to offer up to God. And then let us reap the dividends of joy and peace that only creating can bring.

For Reflection and Discussion

1. Do you agree that using your creativity helps alleviate stress?

2. Do you feel you are fully utilizing your creativity?

3. Do you agree that "when we have fashioned something that bears the stamp of our own brain or hand, we have done the most satisfying thing in the world"?

4. Have you ever personally fashioned something that brought you joy?

5. Which of the three obstacles to creativity mentioned in this chapter most applies to you?

6. Do you think that our culture emphasizes "left brain" functions to the neglect of the "right brain"?

7. What have you always wanted to create? If you have yet to create it, what is holding you back?

What good will it be for a man if he gains the whole world, yet forfeits his soul? Or what can a man give in exchange for his soul?

Matthew 16:26

"Even a millionaire would in actual fact be 'better off' if he chose liberation instead of the plastic world of material wealth. If he exchanged wealth, status, and power for love, creativity, and liberation, he would be far happier; he would make a good bargain."

Charles Reich, *The Greening of America*

5

TREASURING TRINKETS

*J*ohn Claypool, in one of his sermons, tells a parable about a young man who was applying for a job. As a part of the application process, the young man had to take an aptitude test. He arrived at the appointed time, was given instructions about the test, and then was ushered into the testing room.

Immediately, though, the young man became enamored with the utensils at his disposal: He straightened the paper on the desk, sharpened his pencils and shined his chair. In fact, he became so engrossed in the material around him he never got around to taking the test! When time was up and the tests were collected, he had nothing to show for his efforts but a neat desk, finely sharpened pencils and an immaculate chair.

Needless to say, he didn't get the job.

That parable, when aimed at our day-to-day activities, has an all too obvious point: We fritter away our lives on nonessentials and forget the reason God put us here. And, like the young man in the testing room, we'll have little of lasting significance to show when our "time is up."

In the Throes of Things

Let me tell you a story. . . .

Mark and Karen married during their senior year in college. They had dated for two years and were certain the relationship would work. Besides, they were both committed Christians and knew their marriage would be God-centered. The wedding was a gala occasion, attended by several hundred family members and friends. The match, everybody agreed, was made in heaven.

After college, Mark got a job with an engineering firm. The pay wasn't overwhelming, but he loved the work and saw considerable potential for advancement. Karen worked for awhile too—as a receptionist at a bank—until she became pregnant eighteen months after the wedding. Mark and Karen fared surprisingly well during this "get acquainted" stage of their marriage and knew without reservation they were in God's will. They lived in a small, two-bedroom apartment, drove a compact car, ate many more hot dogs than T-bones and generally enjoyed life together.

When Sarah was born, Karen quit her job at the bank and became a full-time mother. Mark got a hefty pay raise, so her salary was hardly missed, and the threesome thrived. Sarah was a delight to her parents—a blue-eyed, blonde miracle whose every tooth and step were meticulously charted in a baby book.

Two years later, Jason was born. The apartment was too crowded for a family of four, so Mark and Karen bought a new house in a nearby subdivision. They took several thousand dollars from their savings account and made the move with no real financial strain.

Of course, their compact car was no longer adequate either; a larger, roomier model had to be purchased. Then, too, the house had to have curtains, a refrigerator, a fence, and a few other things to make it really liveable. Mark and Karen secured loans at a local bank for all of the things they needed. For the first time in their married lives they began to feel financially strapped. Mark was getting annual raises, though, and every bill was met, every need satisfied.

The children grew as all healthy children grow, and there seemed to be a constant need for shoes, clothes, toys, food, and furniture. When Sarah started kindergarten, Karen had to have transportation, so Mark presented her with the keys to a new mini-van on their seventh Christmas together. Certainly they would have to watch their budget, but didn't all young families have to pinch pennies at times?

Mark was promoted again—his salary was now nearly double what it was when he started—but the cost of living seemed to eat up his monthly paycheck. The mortgage, the car notes, the monthly bills, the kids' needs, and the family entertainment took every penny. When a large, unexpected medical problem suddenly surfaced, Karen volunteered to go back to work to ease the burden. She enrolled Jason in a day-care center and got a job at a savings-and-loan. After school, Sarah was dropped off at the day-care center, and Karen picked up both children when she got off work.

Surprisingly, the financial pressure didn't subside even with two incomes. Every month, it seemed, some money-eating monster reared its ugly head and devoured any surplus funds. Mark worked, Karen worked, the kids went to school and day-care, and life grew more and more hectic. There just wasn't time to picnic in the park, fly kites, read books.

Mark and Karen paid their bills, maintained their possessions, stayed active in their church, and did their best to foster a healthy family environment. To the outside observer they appeared to be happy people raising happy children. But the joy they knew early in their marriage was slipping away and, sometimes in rare moments of solitude, they wondered how they could step off this mad merry-go-round. They wondered, in fact, how they had ever gotten on the merry-go-round in the first place.

An Empty Promise

If they don't get off the merry-go-round soon, Mark and Karen will stumble into mid-life just like millions of other "happy people with happy children." Mark will be a "successful" engineer raking in a lot of money. He will also be secretly depressed and quietly disillusioned. Karen will be a "successful" working mother who feels estranged from her husband and children and, perhaps more tragically, from herself. They will have an abundance of material things, but they will not have abundant life. Their acquisition of things will make them thirsty for more things, and their thing-thirst will never be quenched. Material things, like too-sweet orange soda pop, always promise more thirst-satisfaction than they deliver.

What Mark and Karen have succumbed to is the empty promise of materialism. This alluring promise says that our personal joy is directly proportional to the number of goods we possess. Amazingly, Christian people swallow this myth as readily as atheists. Churches are filled with Marks and Karens who are furiously gaining the whole world but slowly paying with their souls, penny by penny.

The myth of materialism, while promising ultimate human fulfillment, actually produces ultimate human stress. The more things we have, the more we want. The more things we have, the more time and money we have to spend maintaining them. The more things we have, the harder we have to work to sustain our lofty standard of living. The more things we have, the faster the merry-go-round whirls, until life is, finally, nauseating.

In the Gospels, Jesus reminds us how dangerous our possessions are. He doesn't say material things are *evil*, but that material things are *seductive*. They tend to consume us, to become our priority, to squeeze God out of our lives: "No one can serve two masters. Either he will hate the one and love the other, or he will be devoted to one and despise the other. You cannot serve both God and Money" (Matt. 6:24). The enemy that lures us away from God, Jesus says, does not always come as an obvious villain intent on demolishing our faith. It comes, instead, as seemingly harmless paper and coin. But paper and coin and the power they bring can easily become the god, the ruling force of our lives.

I do not think it a coincidence that immediately after His statement about the impossibility of serving two masters, Jesus launches out on a discourse about worry. Money and worry are constant traveling companions, and when money becomes god, anxiety is an inevitable result. Show me a person whose life is wrapped around by money, and I will show you a person eaten up with stress.

But Christ bids us to dethrone things—to simply trust in God again, and then reap the joyful benefits. Don't fret about what you will eat or drink or wear, but seek first the kingdom of God. Don't worry about tomorrow. Instead, live with peace today and know that strength for tomorrow is there if you need it. Be like the birds of the air and the lilies of the field; don't wring your hands or spend sleepless nights troubled about the future. Trust God and be at peace.

Am I a Materialist?

Doesn't that sound good? Isn't that what you want—to trust God and be at peace? I think it is.

But I also know that getting that message of peace to your heart is not easy. I know, too, that all of us have to make some hard decisions about our possessions. The line that separates us from materialism is not so clearly marked and, frankly, we're not sure when we've crossed it. (To ease my conscience, I usually define a materialist as anyone having a higher standard of living than I do!)

Let's be honest: Most of us have no immediate plans to sell all we have and give the money to the poor, as Jesus commanded the rich young ruler. We would admire any-

67

one with that kind of dedication, but we're quite content, thank you, with our cars, houses, televisions, air conditioners and stuffed pantries. Given a choice between having a lot or having a little, most of us would have no trouble making our decision.

I have some sermons in my repertoire that scald people for their materialistic selfishness. I have preached messages that sent everyone dragging from the sanctuary, burdened with guilt for hoarding so much stuff. But, lately, I have glimpsed my own hypocrisy and am now more hesitant to pronounce doom on those "rich sinners." More Sundays than I care to admit, I issued those tirades against materialism and then, attired in my spiffy three-piece suit, climbed into my new car and drove my family to the cafeteria for lunch. I count it an offering of grace that the members of my church didn't laugh at me to my face.

While it is easy to preach heavy, "prophetic" sermons against materialism, it is not nearly so easy to deal with the ambiguities and questions we find in the real world. Here are just a few of the facts with which we have to grapple:

- We *do* have a lot of things.
- We *do* get pleasure from the things we possess.
- We *do* need to give liberally to "kingdom causes."
- We *do* need to feel guilty when we become self-absorbed.
- We *do* need to be free of unnecessary, legalistic guilt.
- We *do* need to chart our own course, under God's leadership, for spending our money.
- We *do* need to be aware that at some fuzzy point there is a line where we cross over into materialism.
- We *do* need to take the scriptural mandates about money seriously.
- We *do* need to live with contagious joy.

I have wrestled quite a bit with those truths. I have never been wealthy, but I have never been poor either. I grew up in a middle-class home and have stayed in that same niche all of my life. We currently live in a small brick

68

house in the suburbs, have carpet on the floor, steaks in the freezer, and two cars in the driveway. We have enough money to keep the kids in blue jeans and tennis shoes and to buy Easter outfits every year. We eat out at least once a week and are not so hard-pressed we can't take in a baseball game or a movie. In other words, we are a fairly typical middle-class American family.

So, how do we know if we've fallen prey to materialism? To be frank, we probably won't really know for a certainty in this life. When the books are finally balanced, we may discover that we have lived rather narcissistic lives, callous to the cries of others. We may yet learn that it was indeed sin to put new carpet in the living room and to dress all the windows in expensive mini-blinds. When the test is over, we may learn to our dismay that we have spent far too much time straightening paper and sharpening pencils. On the other hand, there's also the possibility that we could live on a shoestring and yet have a materialistic mindset.

Dancing to a Different Tune

We each have to chart our own course when it comes to stewardship, and I am skeptical of standardized plans. But perhaps our family's experience can serve as a beginning point for those who are struggling with the budget. Perhaps our philosophy can help the Marks and Karens of the world to begin rethinking theirs.

Some of its key ingredients are as follows:

Dance to a different tune. We do our best as a family to stay off the materialistic merry-go-round (though, to be sure, not always with success). When it comes to our investments, we are not listening to E. F. Hutton; we are trying to listen to God. We believe Waylon Jennings is right: "This successful life we're livin's got us feudin' like the Hatfields and McCoys." We have no plans to give up and move to an old run-down house, but we do think Waylon is on target when he concludes: "Maybe it's time we got back to the basics of love." To be Christian with regard to money puts us at odds with popular philosophies and priorities, but the first step in fashioning our own philosophy is to take Paul's counsel and "not conform any longer to the pattern of this world" (Rom. 12:2). We will try our best to dance to a different tune.

Give at least a tithe. I know there are those who say that the tithe is strictly an Old Testament concept—but it is still a good place to begin when planning a budget. The tithe is built on a solid theological premise: We who know a lavish God cannot be hoarders; we must give a part of what we earn to care for others. At least a tenth of what we make is to be invested in the needs of people. If our family budget will not allow us to tithe, we know we have been ensnared by materialism. If our budget is so loaded we can't spare ten percent to feed the hungry or spread the Good News, something is sadly askew.

Save every month. The old formula that called for giving a tenth and saving a tenth still makes good sense. While our family does not routinely deposit ten percent of the paycheck in a savings account, we do try to put something in savings every month. When it is time for another car or a refrigerator or a new roof, we don't have to sniff anxiously for loans or take on extra jobs.

Learn to be content. Once material things are seen as the orange soda pop they are, we can be satisfied with what we already have. Acquiring more stuff simply will not add up to the abundant life. As long as the old car gets down the road, we don't need a new one. As long as the house provides us basic comfort, we'd be foolish to sink into debt for a more expensive one. As long as the gadgets we have now function reasonably well, why should we clutter our lives with more gadgets? We are learning to be content and to give thanks for the prosperity we already enjoy.

Those four ideas will not win any prizes for either originality or profundity. Other financial schemes are more impressive and complicated. The one thing this simple plan has in its favor does carry considerable weight: It works—at least for our family. In trying to dance to a different tune, give at least a tithe, save every month, and practice the art of contentment, we are taking small steps that are leading us to freedom.

The Freedom to Be

Erich Fromm has written a book with a title that expresses with stark simplicity the choice we all face: *To Have or to Be?* We can invest our lives in having or being, in purchasing "goodies" or developing character, in straightening paper and sharpening pencils or in taking the test.

Fromm, like Jesus, encourages us to opt for "being." Our society's choice "to have," he contends, has only led to disillusionment:

> We are a society of notoriously unhappy people: lonely, anxious, depressed, destructive, dependent— people who are glad when we have killed the time we are trying so hard to save.
>
> Ours is the greatest social experiment ever made to solve the question whether pleasure . . . can be a satisfactory answer to the problem of human existence. For the first time in history the satisfaction of the pleasure drive is not only the privilege of a minority but is possible for more than half the population. The experiment has already answered the question in the negative.

Fromm's conclusion sounds remarkably like Jesus in the Sermon on the Mount: "Greed and peace preclude each other."

Can we climb off the merry-go-round? Can we flee greed and move toward peace? Certainly. But only if we are willing to invest our lives in something other than the stock market, other than a European vacation, other than a bigger house in a more exclusive neighborhood. Jumping off a whirling merry-go-round, remember, is a jump that

71

calls for a considerable amount of gumption. We may never make the leap because it is such a gamble.

In his book *Christ the Tiger*, Thomas Howard aptly depicts the risk we must be willing to take:

> How is a man to opt for a kind of life in which he stands to lose everything? I mean, if you want to get a seat on the subway you have to push for it. "So much the worse" for the one who has to stand. And if you want the ecstasies, you have to go flat out to accumulate them. How can a man be expected to opt out of everything that looks important on the chance that there is more to it than meets the eye? It is too great a risk.
>
> Perhaps that is what is asked, I thought. Perhaps there is no escape from risk. Perhaps there is no explanation offered for the staggering ambiguities, nor any answer given to the agonizing questions. Perhaps a man is asked to opt with all his might for authenticity. Perhaps the greatest thing is to respond, with as much integrity as he can summon, to the cues. There *are* some—in his own consciousness, in his art, in his world. And there is this great light that has appeared in the murk, like a morning star. It is there, silent and glorious. An odd road marker. But perhaps a man is asked to go that way on the supposition that it is not all a ghastly cheat.
>
> Yes, perhaps that is what is asked.

To take that risk, to opt for authenticity, to respond to the cues, to follow the light, to bet even our money on God—that *is* what is asked. And I believe it is the way to peace.

For Reflection and Discussion

1. Do you think the story of Mark and Karen is a common one in our society? Is it in any way your story?

2. Why are possessions dangerous?

3. Do you agree with this statement: "Show me a person whose life is wrapped around by money, and I will show you a person eaten up with stress"?

4. Do you ever wonder if you've succumbed to materialism? How can you know?

5. Do you and your family have a philosophy of stewardship? What are the major tenets of your philosophy?

6. What do you think about tithing? Do you think modern Christians should make tithing a priority?

7. Do you ever feel you are on a merry-go-round? If so, how can you get off?

8. Are you willing to bet even your hard-earned money on God?

9. How much of your stress is caused by greed?

Come to me, all you who are weary and burdened, and I will give you rest. Take my yoke upon you and learn from me, for I am gentle and humble in heart, and you will find rest for your souls. For my yoke is easy and my burden is light.

Matthew 11:28–30

"Let the squares on our calendars be meadows for dancing."

Lewis Smedes, *How Can It Be All Right When Everything Is All Wrong?*

6

THE BUMBLEBEE SYNDROME

A couple of years ago, a friend sent me a poem which I consider a remarkably accurate snapshot of hectic life in the late 1980's. It reads:

This is the age
Of the half-read page
And the mad dash
With the nerves tight
The plane hop
With the brief stop
The lamp tan
In a short span
The Big Shot
In a good spot
And the brain strain
And the heart pain
And the cat naps
Till the spring snaps
And the fun's done.

Only later did I learn that those words were penned by a woman named Virginia Brasier and published in *The*

Saturday Evening Post on May 28, 1949. That lyrical snap-shot of contemporary life was nearly forty years old!

I can't help but wonder what Virginia Brasier would write today. If she thought it was a brain-straining, heart-paining time in 1949, nerves were tight and springs were snapping back then, what words would she use to describe the emotional state of people in the late eighties?

The Crammed Calendar

Most of my weekdays start pretty much the same. I wake before the rest of the family, make coffee, and read the newspaper in glorious solitude. Then I awaken the rest of the clan, we eat breakfast together, dress and head to our various destinations.

I'm usually the first one at the office, so it's my lot to make the coffee there, too. While the water is bubbling through the coffee maker, I find what is called my "executive planner," which normally lies among the clutter on my desk. My "executive planner" is actually a pocket calendar book with plenty of space to put reminders, notes and appointments on each day of the month. As the coffee gurgles, I use this time to remember my appointments and plan my daily agenda.

Today's reminders were fairly typical: 5:30—baseball game, 7—meet with Bill and Larry, 8—council meeting. Tomorrow's space, I notice, tells me: 10—see Mrs. Smith, 8—see Frank & Dorothy. Of course there will be a multitude of other tasks to perform, tasks so routine I need no reminder to do them. But I learned years ago to write down all of the not-so-routine things and to begin each day with my calendar-planner. The few times I've neglected this part of the daily regimen, I have inevitably missed a meeting or muffed an opportunity.

Each of us should have a daily planner, I think, if only to remind ourselves that *we* are in charge of our time. Those spaces in my planner are totally *blank* when I get it the first of every year. It is up to me to set my own priorities and plan an agenda. The calendar is neutral; it can neither bless nor tyrannize. The blessing or tyranny comes only from the pen of the one who fills those spaces with scribbling.

We typically try to weasel out of responsibility whenever possible, so this is important to remember. We are prone to sigh, "I just don't have time," as if time or God or who-knows-what-else is responsible for our hectic, misdirected lives. The truth is: We have as much time as anyone else. We have more than enough time to fashion a life brimming with love, laughter, God, creativity, purpose and peace. If we don't have those things, if we are exhausted and unfulfilled, we can't honestly blame it on the calendar, or our spouse, or our kids, or our "particular situation." If that poem of Virginia Brasier's describes us, it is only because we have *chosen* a life of "quick hashes and mad dashes." If the calendar is crammed with a futile flurry of schemes and activities, it is only because we have written those schemes and activities there in our own handwriting. The open squares on our calendars start out as meadows for dancing.

The Day of the Dabbler

Perhaps the most accurate symbol for most of us is the bumblebee. We flit from one activity to another, dabbling in everything and concentrating on nothing. We buzz here and there, stay constantly on the go, desperately desiring to be busy. Mark Twain once said, "Civilization is a limitless multiplication of unnecessary necessities." Nowhere is that more evident than in our personal management of time. Ernest Campbell says, in *Locked in a Room with Open Doors*, "The man to be pitied is the man who believes in everything just a little bit, the miscellaneous man who has never brought the tattered fragments of his life under the command of a single voice, or gathered his abilities around a single passion." Or, I might add, purged his calendar of all meaningless fluff, activities that contribute little to either the world or our own joy.

Perhaps you are as besieged with "good causes" as I am. The opportunities are staggering. I "ought" to coach Little League, lead a scout troop, collect funds for the heart association, attend church and denominational meetings, spend time with the children, pursue a fitness program, support my favorite politician, take my wife out at least once a week, work in the P.T.A., socialize with friends, combat pornography, give blood at the blood drive, help stamp out illiteracy, adopt a pet, and give money to at least a dozen worthwhile charities. Somewhere along the way I also have to work forty hours a week, write books, eat, sleep, mow the grass, maintain the cars, clean the garage, and spend time alone with God. Chances are, you have a similar list of "necessary" things to do.

Who can deny the validity of any of those things? What caring person among us could turn a deaf ear to any of those causes? (And who would have the audacity to call any of those things "meaningless fluff"?) Because we *recognize* the good, we feel *obligated* to have a go at all of them. Thus the bumblebee syndrome—frantically buzzing around a dozen different flowers, trying with all sincerity to make a difference in the world.

The bumblebee syndrome really only accomplishes two things. It *diminishes* our impact on the world, and it *creates* a ton of stress. The miscellaneous man desires effective involvement; what he gets is the frustration of busyness. The bumblebee approach to life has been tried by millions of good Christians and found to be a sure way to ungodly exhaustion.

Until we sift through that ponderous pile of "good causes" and settle on a few that truly claim our heart, we are destined for misery. Sometimes our commitment to Christ demands not that we do more but that we do *less*— that we drop some "good causes" to embrace what, for us,

78

are better causes. If we don't simplify our schedule, our testimony will begin to echo what Tim Hansel said of his own in *When I Relax I Feel Guilty*:

> I was dominated by "should's," "ought to's," and "must's." I would awaken unrefreshed in the morning, with a tired kind of resentment, and hurry through the day trying to uncover and meet the demands of others. Days were not lived but endured. I was exhausted trying to be a hope constantly rekindled for others, straining to live up to their images of me. I had worked hard to develop a reputation as one who was concerned, available and involved—now I was being tyrannized by it. Often I was more at peace in the eyes of others than in my own.

A Modest Plan for Changing the World

My own battle with the daily planner is still being waged. I am still in the process of discovering those causes that are to be priority for me. So far, these have bobbed to the surface:

Pastoring—I am the pastor of a suburban church and have been for the past twelve years. Naturally, this church stakes a large claim on my life. To do my job and fulfill my calling, I must study, visit, plan worship services, counsel, meet with committees, not to mention a host of indispensable tasks like emptying trash cans, setting up chairs and running old copy machines.

Family—My wife and two children cannot be neglected. I *will* take Sherry to breakfast every Thursday morning. I *will* be at the kids' ball games and school activities. The whole family *will* worship together every Sunday and vacation together every summer. I *will* attend to the physical, emotional and spiritual needs of my family.

Writing—I cannot be "me" without putting a pen to paper and trying to express my insides. E. B. White once described writing as an affliction, as "something that raises up on you, as a welt." For better or worse, I have the affliction and spend a lot of time wrestling with words, type-writers, and publishing companies. I am not a particularly disciplined writer. I don't, as some writers claim to do, have a goal of writing a certain number of pages every day. I write in spasmodic spurts, but seldom does a week go by that I haven't hurled words at paper to see if any of them make sense.

Reading—I have already confessed to being a "booka-holic." Books give me hours of enjoyment. They feed my spirit. They give me ideas to preach. They allow me to escape periodically to a better world. Because I find reading valuable for my own personal growth, I try to read a book a week.

Running—I spend most of my day behind a desk, or in a car, or in my favorite recliner. Running gives me one activity every day that raises both my heart rate and my spirit. I run at least three miles a day through our subdi-vision, and find that I need this time both because it enables me to stay physically fit and because it gives me opportunity to flee (literally) the pressures of my usual routine. "On the run" I can think, pray, wave at neighbors, smell hamburg-ers being cooked on outdoor grills, and liberate the child within me that wants to play.

Those five things have become priorities for me. I can concentrate on those five "causes" and build a life that has both purpose and flexibility. They do not demand so much of me that I run myself ragged. If another cause rears its head and begs for attention, I have the freedom to consider it. Recently, for instance, the opportunity to coach my son's baseball team presented itself. I accepted and spent many hours during three months teaching the red-and-gold Car-dinals how to bunt, slide and turn a double play. If another pressing need arises, my schedule is loose enough that I can weigh its claim on me and act accordingly.

But I will not be a bumblebee. Recently I rejected a denominational responsibility and an offer to play on a softball team simply because they don't fit my current priorities. I cannot do everything. And as a result, I have had to limit my participation in many worthwhile endeavors. I am doing my best to avoid what Thomas Kelly described as "the poverty of life that comes from an over-abundance of opportunity." All of us, I suspect, have an over-abundance of opportunity. What we must zealously guard against is that bedraggled poverty of life that furtively tags along with it.

What I have learned in sorting through my own bundle of abundant opportunities is, I would guess, the testimony of all former bumblebees: The way to change the world is to give yourself with abandon to one small corner of it.

Answering the Activists

Is there a voice inside you protesting such a simple agenda? Perhaps you are thinking: "That's an escapist, narcissistic philosophy if ever I've heard one. Where in your Christian commitment is concern for world hunger, world peace, apartheid, abortion, poverty, child abuse and political corruption? Where is personal evangelism, prayer, ecumenical interest and support for your denomination? Don't you know the follower of Jesus is called to be involved in the world? Don't you think your five priorities are flimsy and inadequate in a world with such monumental problems?"

Yes, I know. Pastoring, tending a family, writing, reading and running do seem tame amid such chaos.

I offer a two-pronged rebuttal: First, I am called to be faithful and, second, I am called to grab on to "the near edge." Lewis Smedes defined faithfulness as finding out "what you are here to take care of, and then give it your best shot." We are to discover those causes that we love, or feel a tugging toward, and then give ourselves unreservedly to them. For me, I must give those five priorities I've mentioned my best shot. Failing to attend to any of them would be moving away from faithfulness. If an activist derides my choices, I can only answer that to the best of my admittedly poor discernment I am trying to be faithful.

When I say I am trying to grab on to "the near edge," I mean that *my* church, *my* family, *my* writing, *my* intellectual growth, *my* attempt to be physically fit all impinge, in some small way, on the whole world. And the only way, or the best way, I can impact the world is to tidy up my small part of it. We are often guilty of promoting big causes while neglecting little people, of loving the world, for example, while our families are falling apart. I, for one, must cast my lot with Wendell Berry, who writes, "A couple who make a good marriage and raise healthy, morally competent children are serving the world's future more directly and surely than any political leader, though they never utter a public word."

I am not advocating that we shun all involvement with big causes. Let us join groups, write letters, contribute money, and do whatever else is necessary to rid the world of evil. But we don't have to be guilt-ridden, time-tyrannized people in the process. We can be faithful to what we perceive as God's voice within us. We can grab "the near edge" and express our love there. And we can be relaxed and free.

How Long Has it Been. . . ?

I really believe that. We *can* be relaxed and free. We want that, and I believe God wants that, too. So it's time to put some seed into the ground that will produce that.

How long has it been since you had time to talk with your spouse and children, to dream with them about the future, to listen to their hurts and hopes?

How long has it been since you spent time alone with God—and enjoyed it?

How long has it been since you laughed until you cried?

How long has it been since you privately wept for joy

because God is so good and life is such a sacred gift?

How long has it been since you "frittered away" a day—puttering in the yard, building a model airplane, painting a picture—and not felt guilty about it?

How long has it been since you had time to help a friend or neighbor?

How long has it been since you lost your "self" because you were having so much fun?

If you are an average, uptight Christian, I can tell you the answer to most of those questions: Too long.

We who have been called to abundant life have somehow entered into a life of frenzy. We have crowded our calendars with good activities, but lost our joy doing it. We live at such a pace that our energy level is low and our blood pressure is high. And like those sad fans W. P. Kinsella describes in his baseball novel, *Shoeless Joe,* we are becoming people "who have withered and sickened of the contrived urgency of their lives."

The good news, though, is that the daily planner *is* firmly in our possession. We can even yet make it an instrument of blessing. We can erase or add at our own discretion and do with tomorrow whatever we choose.

Who knows? We may make those squares on our calendars meadows for dancing after all.

For Reflection and Discussion

1. Do you ever feel you just don't have enough time to do those things you think are important?

2. List below five causes or activities you think should be priority for you.

   1.

   2.

   3.

   4.

   5.

3. Which of those in your list are you neglecting? Why?

4. What do you think of the statement, "Being faithful means to find out what you are here to take care of and then give it your best shot"? What are you here to take care of? Are you giving it your best shot?

5. Do you need to grab on to "the near edge"? Who or what close to you needs your love and attention?

6. Do you think it is possible in our frenzied world to be relaxed and free? Do you think of yourself as relaxed and free?

7. How much of your stress is caused by an overcrowded calendar?

Dear children, let us not love with words or tongue but with actions and in truth.

1 John 3:18

"The formula for finding your own, primary mission is here:
Put down this book. Walk outside your house, trailer, or apartment. Look in through a window. Now you see where Christ has sent you. Serving starts where you are. If you understand that your mission to the faces at your table, no matter how few, ranks in importance with the mission of a great evangelist to crowds of thousands, then you have begun to understand Love."

Paula D'Arcy, *Where the Wind Begins*

7

STARVING THE PLANTS

*J*ust now it's spring. We have been performing a rite customary to all people who wish to celebrate the season properly: We have been planting flowers in the yard. More accurately, I admit that my wife, Sherry, has done the planting. We have worked out a nice arrangement: She plants the flowers; I admire them and brag on her horticultural skills.

Most of the flowers she plants come with little tags, listing all the pertinent information—how far apart the plants should be, how much sun and water are needed, how the mature flower looks. These pointed tags can be stuck in the dirt to serve as a constant reminder of the care each flower needs.

In the glove compartment of both of my cars I carry an owner's manual. Without one, who would know how to operate the air conditioner or check the brake fluid? Perhaps those with mechanical expertise could handle it, but what about those of us who are "mechanical illiterates," who barely know where to add the oil?

Those tags on the plants and those owner's manuals in

the glove compartments serve a vital purpose. They spell out the necessary advice for growing healthy flowers and keeping cars running efficiently. The only variable is our willingness to heed the directions.

Mandatory Wrist Tags

I hereby propose that from this time forth all babies be strapped with a wrist tag at birth. It makes no sense to me that we should have simple, printed instructions for flowers and cars and absolutely none for human beings. So, when a baby is pushed screaming into this world, let us immediately lash a tag onto that baby's wrist, a tag that says something like this:

> For proper development, this person must be touched, kissed, talked to, listened to, prayed for, and given utmost attention. Unless this person is the object of someone's delight, this person will wither and die.

I would even go so far as to suggest that the wrist tag be worn all through life.

When said person reaches the age of five and goes off to kindergarten, everyone—parents, grandparents, teachers, principal—can look at the tag and remember what it takes for a kindergartner to survive the new and frightening rigors of school life.

When said person is about to begin junior high, parents and siblings and friends can look at the tag again and refresh their memories: This gangling, silly, obnoxious, confused child must be touched, kissed, talked to, listened to, prayed for and given utmost attention. The information on the wrist tag, you see, is as true for adolescents as it is for infants.

About the time this same individual gets married, let's make it a requirement for everyone to read the tag again. And remember: If this one is going to have a joy-filled marriage, these directions must be followed carefully.

When our person enters mid-life and faces the now famous mid-life crisis, it would behoove us to read the instructions again and to remember that people in their forties are pondering, perhaps for the first time in their life, their own coming death. Often, they are also struggling with teenage children, broken dreams, job dissatisfaction and a once-youthful body that is sagging in all the wrong places.

Years later, when this person checks in to the nursing home, we should read the tag once more. And once more we could remember: Old people need to be touched, kissed, talked to, listened to, prayed for and given utmost attention. From nursery to nursing home the species called "human being" grows and thrives only in an environment of caring. All of us need to be loved with a particular, focused kind of love.

Filling Love Tanks

I seriously doubt that my wrist tag idea will catch on. (Though when I proposed the idea from the pulpit one recent Sunday morning, thirty or forty people showed up for our worship service that evening wearing homemade wrist tags. We had a lot of hugging after the service that night!) Delivery room procedure will no doubt continue pretty much as is.

In lieu of mandatory wrist tags, perhaps we could all memorize 1 John 3:18: "Let us not love with words or tongue but with actions and in truth." Those fourteen words would remind us of our primary charge as followers of Jesus Christ. We are not just to talk about love, believe in love, or advocate love. We are to *do* love. We are to roll up our sleeves and start loving. We are to shower those closest to us with our delight and affection.

In my earlier book, *Dancing to Zion*, I suggested that every person comes into this world with an invisible love tank. When that love tank gets low, terrible things start happening. People with a lack of love in their lives get depressed, anxious, angry and even suicidal. Human beings are created to "run on love," and when the love tank is not regularly refueled the results are devastating. A plant without water will wilt and die. A car without gasoline will sputter to a standstill. And people without love will always find life a dreadful experience.

Those of us who have chosen to follow Christ have chosen a life of filling love tanks. That is our primary ministry. When asked about the greatest commandment, remember, Christ pinpointed it as loving God and loving people. We Christians are not primarily thinkers, prayers, or persuaders, though we should be all of those things. But *primarily* we are love-tank-fillers. We have been given the delightful, demanding assignment of energizing other people with love.

A Parable to Consider

Here's a parable to reflect upon:

A young man ran out of gas one hot afternoon in the middle of a desert in Arizona. He was too far from civilization to walk for help, so his only hope was that a passing motorist would stop and lend him aid. Unfortunately, passing motorists were few and far between on this isolated stretch of desert highway. The young man sat dejectedly in his car and prayed that some caring soul would pass his way.

Eventually, a car did appear down that lonely ribbon of road. To the young man's great joy, the driver saw his plight and pulled up beside him. He inquired as to the young man's problem, and when he heard it was a lack of gasoline he launched into a scholarly discussion of the various kinds of gasoline available. It was obvious that this driver was schooled in the chemical properties of gasoline and spoke authoritatively of octane levels and the difference between leaded and unleaded fuel. After delivering his impressive discourse and prescribing the ideal fuel for the young man's car, he went merrily on his way. As he pulled away, the young man noticed the personalized plates on his car: T-H-I-N-K-E-R.

An hour or so passed and a second car pulled over. The driver was meek and kind and, upon hearing the problem, offered assuring words of comfort. He expressed genuine concern for the young man's dilemma and then intoned a lengthy prayer on his behalf: He asked God to smile upon this difficult situation and to fill the empty gas tank with fuel from heaven. Then he got back in his car and sped down the highway. As the young man watched the car pull away, he saw printed on the license plate this word: P-R-A-Y-E-R. The young man slumped despondently in his car.

To his surprise and delight, however, a third car pulled alongside him in just a matter of minutes. The driver jumped out, quickly ascertained the young man's plight and launched into an animated exhortation. First he chided him for his carelessness, then outlined a four-point program for driving a car successfully. When he finished, he too took off down the road. The bewildered young man saw that his license plate read: P-E-R-S-U-A-D-E-R.

In despair the young man looked helplessly up and down the desert highway. An hour passed. No cars came into view. All the young man could do was wait—and hope against hope that help would come.

Finally, a fourth car approached. The young man's heart did flip-flops as the car pulled up next to his. The driver inquired as to the problem, and then pulled a five-gallon gas can from his trunk. He emptied the can into the young man's tank, and waited until he was sure the car would start. Then, smiling, he went on his way. The young man hardly had time to shout a thank-you. He did glimpse the car's license plates, but they were not personalized and he couldn't quite make out the letters. With great gratitude and relief, the young man shifted his car into gear and rumbled down the highway.

Now I ask you: Which of these motorists was the young man's neighbor? And, which do you suppose, had read 1 John 3:18?

Narrowing the Focus

The young man in that story may be your husband, or wife, or child, or father, or mother. The one who is stranded out there in an emotional desert is possibly someone close to us.

Why is it that we so often neglect those closest to us? Husbands, wives, children, parents and friends wither emotionally because of indifference. Only when we start pouring some narrowly focused love into their love tanks will they come to life again.

The trouble with most of our love is that it is too broad. Real love is always extremely specific. Better to go to a ball game with one freckle-faced boy than to preach a dozen sermons on the Good Samaritan. Better to spend one loving weekend in seclusion with your spouse than to lead a multitude of seminars on building a good marriage. Better, I must remind myself, to take your daughter out to eat on her birthday than to write sentimental words about love in a book.

Several years ago I was reading Bruce Larson's book, *The One and Only You,* and came across a story that grabbed my attention. I think it grabbed me because it is so foreign to my own safe, practical approach to life:

> I have a great friend down in Montgomery, Alabama, and a few years ago he told me an unforgettable story of a summer vacation he had planned for his wife and children. He was unable to go himself because of business, but he helped them plan every day of a camping trip in the family station wagon from Montgomery all the way to California, up and down the West Coast, and then back to Montgomery.
> He knew their route exactly and the precise time they

would be crossing the Great Divide. So, my friend arranged to fly himself out to the nearest airport and hire a car and driver to take him to a place where every car must pass. He sat by the side of the road for several hours waiting for the sight of that familiar station wagon. When it came into view, he stepped out on the road and put his thumb out to hitchhike a ride with the family who assumed he was 3,000 miles away.

I said to him, "Coleman, I'm surprised they didn't drive off the road in terror or drop dead of a heart attack. What an incredible story. Why did you go to all that trouble?"

"Well, Bruce," he said, "Someday I'm going to be dead, and when that happens I want my kids and wife to say, 'You know, Dad was a lot of fun.' "

I know, of course, what they will say about me. "You know, Dad was a good guy, but he was awfully uptight about us brushing our teeth and cleaning our rooms." I only hope they will be able to see my antiseptic admonitions as true (albeit warped) expressions of love.

I doubt that I will ever fly 3,000 miles to surprise my family on a vacation. I'd be too afraid they would drive right by and never see me! But I do believe this: That crazy man's heart is in the right place. One foolish, surprising act of love for a few people does more to energize lives than all of the "general concern" in the world.

So Why Don't We Love More Specifically?

The painful questions are: Why don't we do a better job of filling love tanks? Why do we neglect those people God has put in our charge? After sorting through all of the possible responses to those questions, there seem to me two simple answers.

First, we get careless. We know by heart all of that information on the wrist tag. We know that people cannot live abundantly without love. Perhaps what I have written in this chapter is "old hat." But I have written anyway because we all need our memory jogged.

Occasionally, we need someone to tap us on the shoulder and remind us of the indispensability of our love. That baby in the crib will die without our love. That child ambling off to kindergarten cannot navigate the choppy sea of school life without our undivided attention. That surly adolescent needs our touch far more than he will ever admit. That newlywed young woman still needs our care. That poor fool fighting the mid-life blues needs our love as much or more than ever. And that bedridden woman in the nursing home can only go on living if we take delight in her.

At the bare minimum, we ought to read the "great commandment" in Matthew 22 and the admonition in 1 John 3:18 once a week. Those passages would give us a concise refresher course in basic Christianity and remind us that as crucial as it is for us to be thinkers, prayers, and persuaders, it is even more crucial that we be people who actively demonstrate love by our specific actions.

The second reason we do such a pitiful job of loving relates back to the last chapter: We get too busy. The squares on our calendar are too crowded to have room for love.

Love takes time. It can't be sandwiched between work and ball practice and church meetings. To really love those significant people in our lives we will have to spend much time with them. And who, in our hyperactive culture, has the time love demands? If we take the ideas in this chapter to heart, we might have to jump off the ladder of success, cut back on our social life, or forego the summer bowling league. And we will most definitely have to decide that this particular person, or these particular people, will get a bigger chunk of "me" and my time.

Don't let anyone's sweet rhetoric about love fool you. Love is costly. It will cost all of us many a tantalizing space in our executive planner.

Weighing Life in the Balance

When we honestly sift through life's priorities, I think all of us would agree that the quality of our relationships—with God and people—is the truest measure of our lives. When life is weighed in the balance, our relationships of love have far more weight than anything else we can put on the scales. Relationships are the finest treasures we have and well worth the time we must invest in them.

When we begin to concentrate our love on a few people, wonderful things happen all around. Not only are the recipients of our love rejuvenated, but we ourselves begin to experience more joy. Since we are designed and called to love, our attempts to take delight in others, however feeble, fulfill us. There are few situations more joyful than living in an environment where people blossom because they get regular waterings of love. Every group—a family, a classroom, an office, a committee, a church—has an atmosphere that either uplifts or destroys. And the crucial ingredient in any of those groups is the quality of love present there.

There is an old fable about a man who dreamed he was taken on a tour of eternity. First he was taken to hell and shown misery beyond belief. All of the occupants of hell, he noticed, had stiff elbows and were unable to feed themselves. Their desperate attempts to get bread to their mouths resulted only in weeping and gnashing of teeth. Then the dreamer was transported to heaven. There he was surprised to see that all of the occupants of heaven had stiff elbows, too. But never had he seen such peace and joy. For all of the people in heaven were holding out bread, to feed someone else.

That is the way we are to live. That is our calling as followers of Jesus Christ. We are to experience God's love and then in tangible, costly ways hold out love to a few hungry people around us. If we hoard the bread, we deny our calling, starve our friends and family, and sabotage our own peace.

In his book, *Notes to Myself*, Hugh Prather writes,

> If I had only . . . forgotten future greatness
> and looked at the green things and
> the buildings
>   and reached out to those around me
>   and smelled the air
> and ignored the forms and self-styled
> obligations
> and heard the rain on my roof
>   and put my arms around my wife
>   . . .and it's not too late.

Perhaps it's not too late. But the time to begin is today.

For Reflection and Discussion

1. Do you think that every person has an invisible "love tank"? Have there been times in your life when yours was empty?

2. Who among your circle of close acquaintances could be stranded in an emotional desert? What can you do about it?

3. Is it possible that your own family is withering because of your "well-intentioned indifference"? Could you unknowingly be neglecting a family member?

4. Think of some specific things you can do to fill people's "love tanks." List them below.

Person	*Needed Action*
1.	1.
2.	2.
3.	3.
4.	4.

5. What will your family say about you after you're gone? Are you a lot of fun?

6. What keeps you from doing a better job of filling "love tanks"? Carelessness? Busyness? Something else?

7. Is your family withering or blossoming? How about the place where you work? How about your church? Will you begin now to "hold out some bread" to those around you?

You will know the truth, and the truth will set you free.

John 8:32

"*Our view of reality is like a map with which to negotiate the terrain of life. If the map is true and accurate, we will generally know where we are, and if we have decided where we want to go, we will generally know how to get there. If the map is false and inaccurate, we will generally be lost.*"

M. Scott Peck, *The Road Less Traveled*

8

GREAT EXPECTATIONS

I nearly lost my religion one day while trying to change a flat tire. When I referred to myself in the last chapter as a "mechanical illiterate," I wasn't kidding. Mr. Goodwrench I am not. But even *I* can usually manage to change a flat.

This particular day, however, I couldn't get the lugs off the wheel to remove the tire. I've never been known as a muscle man, but I'm no wimp either, and never before had I struggled so hard to get lugs to budge. I grunted. I groaned. I pushed. I pulled. I beat on the lug wrench with a hammer. The lugs wouldn't give. Finally I gave up, left the tire unchanged, and stalked into the house defeated.

Later, I shared my frustration on the telephone with a friend. "Try turning the lugs the other way," he said off-handedly. *That* was a stupid suggestion. Lugs and nuts always tighten when turned in a clockwise direction and loosen when turned in a counterclockwise direction. Every jack-leg mechanic knows that. Nonetheless, in desperation, I went out and gave it a try. I tried to loosen the lug by turning it clockwise. Wonder of wonders, it budged! So did all of the other lugs on the wheel. In a matter of moments, I had the flat tire off and the new one mounted. But I never would have thought to turn those lugs the opposite way unless my friend had suggested it. I just *knew* I was doing it the right way.

In a way, the message of this whole book is "try turning the lugs the other way." But this chapter, in particular, is an invitation to look at the basic suppositions by which we live. Maybe we're going about life the wrong way, with a bunch of wrong expectations. And maybe we'll never fix the flat until we try something new.

Anxiety and False Expectations

In his book, *The Courage to Create,* Rollo May tells of a research assignment he did for his earlier book, *The Meaning of Anxiety.* He took it upon himself to study a group of unmarried pregnant women, young women in their late teens and early twenties living in a shelter home in New York City. May was trying to verify the hypothesis that people who have been rejected by their mothers tend to have a lot of anxiety. He would study these women in the shelter, then try to determine the importance of maternal rejection on a person's anxiety level.

The hypothesis proved true for some in the group. Those young women from middle-class homes fit the theory exactly—high maternal rejection bred high anxiety. Curiously, though, the women from lower-class homes didn't validate the theory at all. The data from discussions and psychological tests revealed these women were rejected but not anxious. In some cases there was total maternal rejection and even abuse, but the anxiety level was low. Why? Why did these lower-class women feel no tension from maternal neglect? Why were they more immune to stress than their middle-class house mates?

May finally concluded the difference in anxiety levels was related to *expectation.* The young women from the middle-class homes expected to be loved, were told in fact that they were loved, but saw no evidence of it. Because their expectations were not met they knew constant frustration. The lower-class women, on the other hand, had no such discrepancy in their minds. They *knew* they were not loved. Their mothers made no pretense of caring for them, so these girls found their supportive relationships elsewhere—in friends or other family members.

The anxiety, in short, stemmed from false expectations. As May writes in the book, "Anxiety comes from not being able to know the world you're in, not being able to orient yourself in your own existence." When expectations are distorted and detached from reality, anxiety always occurs.

Making a Life Map

Look long and hard at your expectations. Have you set yourself up for frustration because your expectations are unrealistic? Have you wandered into misery because your view of reality is cockeyed? Is it possible you're lost because your map was never accurate in the first place?

The finest among us have blind spots. The most adventuresome trailblazers in our midst sometimes stumble into snake pits. That's why we need the Bible, church, books, friends, and family. They point us in the general direction of abundant living.

All of us are making a life map. At birth we started on a journey that continues to this very moment, a journey that has been meticulously mapped and recorded by our brain. Our parents have tremendously affected our view of reality and the kind of map we've drawn. Our school experiences, our successes and failures, our religious training, our friends' remarks, our culture's mores—these things and many more have helped us plot the personal map by which we navigate life. I believe it is not overstating the case to say that the map we carry in our head is the most valuable possession we have.

This map determines how we view God, whether we see Him as fiend or Father. This map tells us which direction to go in our personal relationships, whether to move toward competition or companionship. It points us toward a job, a marriage partner, a personality, a hobby. Indeed, this map is a brain-diagrammed plan for living that we follow every day. We walk its way each day of our lives, and discerning people can see our map if they but watch our feet.

If this map is an accurate representation of reality, the journey will be full of joy. If this map is askew, full of side roads and dead ends, the journey will be constant frustration. The only difference in the young women in the New York shelter, remember, was their map. All of those girls Rollo May studied had maternal rejection. Those with high anxiety just didn't have maternal rejection as a locus on their maps.

The good news is that life maps are never written in indelible ink. The girls in the home can begin now to see reality as it is, to pencil in rejection on their maps (as painful as it is to draw those lines), and to make peace with a rotten past. Nobody is stuck permanently with an outdated map. We can update it at any time, erase some roads that have proven to go nowhere, and sketch in some new trails that just might get us to our destination of joyful living.

In her book, *Where the Wind Begins*, Paula D'Arcy reminds us, "In the end, that's how those who are free become free. They are the few who learn that truth, not pleasure, is the hiding place of joy." It is the truth that sets us free, that sets our toes to tapping. So, periodically, we must take out our map and inspect it for flaws. Especially if we feel we're drifting away from the abundant life do we need to scrutinize our life map and make every effort to update it, to make sure it accurately follows the contours of reality.

With these thoughts in mind, I want to uncover some prevalent false expectations that lead us away from truth. If these expectations are part of our personal map, we are setting ourselves up for pain. Remember, the closer our map is to reality, the better our chances for joy.

The Need for Unanimous Approval

One false idea that plagues many of us, it seems to me, is the belief that we will be universally loved and lauded. Any sane person prefers approval over disapproval. Show me a man or woman who doesn't want approval and I will show you a misfit at best and a psychopath at worst.

But our natural inclination for approval can become so extreme it becomes joy-sapping. We can so worship acclaim that we become human chameleons, changing our colors to adapt to the tastes of whoever we happen to be with at the moment. When we make public opinion our god, we lose our identity, our "self," our uniqueness. In an attempt to buy acceptance, we lose the very thing that is necessary for abundant living—a robust, one-of-a-kind personality that dares to be nothing but itself.

Don't misunderstand and use this section of the book to justify belligerent behavior. Don't make these words say that we can do and be whatever we wish and let the chips fall where they may. If we routinely alienate people, if we're continually a bull in the relational china shop, something is sorely amiss. We can't really blame our poor relationships on "a unique self that others just don't understand."

But for every bull on the rampage through the china shop there are probably a dozen nice, respectable Christian people who are tiptoeing through life so as not to offend anyone. They are following the god of universal approval instead of the God who thundered, "Do not conform any longer to the pattern of this world . . ." (Rom. 12:2). Until they venture into the perilous country of nonconformity, they will stay mired in joyless respectability.

Our task—indeed our Christian witness to the world— is to proclaim Christ through the self that God has made us to be. True, that self is flawed, sinful, in progress. Like the Apostle Paul, we carry this treasure in marred, earthen vessels, but, incredibly, some people need us. Some people will even see God if we dare to display the earthen vessel we are.

I like the analogy Richard Bach uses in *Illusions*:

> Well, . . . we're magnets, aren't we? Not magnets. We're iron, wrapped in copper wire, and whenever we want to magnetize ourselves we can. Pour our inner voltage through the wire, we can attract whatever we want to attract. A magnet is not anxious about how it works. It is itself, and by its nature draws some things and leaves others untouched.

If our map says that everyone will be attracted to us, it is time to update the map. As one of my acquaintances puts it, "It is not appointed unto one man to ring everybody's bell."

I had to come to grips with that myself a few years ago. Not everyone will like my preaching. I know that's hard to believe, but it's true. Not everyone will buy my books. Not everyone will find my personality scintillating. But—and here's the good news in all of this—some will! I will influence *some* people because they like my style, my message, my "me." The magnet does, on surprisingly frequent occasions, do its natural work.

The End of Struggle

A second false ideal that needs to be erased from our maps is the notion that at some glorious moment in the future life will cease to be a struggle. I think many of us dream of a struggle-free existence, of life as a quiet stream with no churning waves or sudden storms.

I've given up the idea that I'll ever escape struggle and stress. For a long time that was on my map, and I was constantly perturbed that I could not achieve the idyllic existence printed there. Now I know better. Life *does* take effort. The race *does* have hurdles. The road down which we travel is *not* Smooth Sailing Lane, our wishes to the contrary.

I think many of us can identify with the psychology professor quoted by Lesley Hazelton in her book, *The Right to Feel Bad*:

> "Being in psychology," he says, "and at my age, and with what I know, I should really have it all together. I *know* what having it all together could be. I *know* what being happy should be. But I just can't do it. It's very frustrating, frustrating and depressing.
>
> " . . . I have a very definite image of some people, somewhere, with impeccable mental health, happy and self-fulfilled, people who don't dwell on things but just go ahead and do them and are immensely successful and likeable. And then there's me, feeling like that little guy in the Jules Feiffer cartoon, the one who's tried everything but only feels at home sitting right in the jaws of the dragon."

We might as well face it: We all find ourselves from time to time in the jaws of that dragon. We fail. We get sick. Our children don't turn out the way we had planned. We don't make the P.G.A. tour or the million dollar round table. At times, like the psychology professor, we feel as if we've taken up permanent residence in the jaws of the dragon.

What those disappointments tell us, though, is that we're human. We're just ordinary earthen vessels given a charge by God not to be perfect but to be faithful. We who know Christ know that every cross has a corresponding resurrection. We who have read the Psalms know that weeping is an undeniable part of life—but after weeping comes a song.

Think again about those girls in Rollo May's study. Those with high anxiety found it hard to admit rejection by their mothers. It is not particularly pleasant to face up to that kind of truth. Nor is it particularly pleasant to face up to a world where struggle is a "given" and pain is ever present. But the sooner we acknowledge the truth, the better our hope for inner peace.

God in a Bottle

Let's probe deeper, for there is a third truth that can correct our map: Our relationship with God is also fraught with struggle. We might have met Him when we were born-again, but the relationship eventually moved beyond that.

Last week, a friend poured out his discouragement about being a Bible study teacher in our church. "We've been studying the second coming of Christ," he said, "and we can't come to any hard and fast conclusions. The more we study, the more confused we become. And then someone in the class asked what happens right after a person dies. So I got out my concordance and tracked down all the references to 'death' in the Bible. Would you believe I never came up with a satisfactory answer? It just seems to me that God ought to provide some explicit answers to such critical questions."

I agree, and at one point in my spiritual pilgrimage I could have given him God's answers to those questions and any others he posed. I had millennial diagrams that spelled out in detail the events surrounding Christ's return. I had prayer, evangelism, ethics and all of the fundamental Christian doctrines in neat compartments. I had a scripture for ever dilemma, a ready answer for life's most puzzling mysteries. My God was in a bottle, and my spiritual life consisted of nothing but principles and proof texts.

At some indefinable point in time, though, God escaped the bottle, and all faith broke loose. The relationship became just that—a true relationship, a searching after One who refuses to be diagrammed like a compound sentence, a yearning for Someone who remains hidden in life's ambiguities, even a protesting to One who refuses to do things my way. In short, I had to learn to live by faith, the one thing we must have to please God.

106

I had to revise my map. I had to redefine God, or better yet, admit my finite dictionary couldn't define the Infinite at all. It was a rough transition. It still is. I wish that the Christian life were an easy way of easy answers, not a hard way of hard faith. But our relationship to God has to be built on a foundation of honesty, or it will not stand when beaten by the winds of life.

The truth is, God is bigger than any bottle we could ever construct.

Where Have All the Perfect People Gone?

A fourth "great expectation" that sets us up for disillusionment, I think, is the belief that people ought to be better than they are. Somewhere out there in the world is a group of great people who can fulfill our lives and be what we need them to be. We know for certain that someday we will stumble onto the perfect marriage partner, the perfect friend, the perfect pastor, the perfect doctor. But when we look at the real live people around us, we are dismayed at their imperfections. They are a rag-tag bunch of folks who show all the signs of being terribly ordinary.

I don't know about your world, but mine is filled with overwhelmingly common people. I know no movie starlets, converse with no geniuses, consult with no experts who have solved life's puzzles.

I thought Ginger was one of "the beautiful people" until she showed up at church one Sunday with a pimple on her cheek, a blister on her lip, and a jaw swollen from recent dental work. I thought Charles was a genius until I really got to know him and found out he knows everything about computers and nothing about the Bible. I thought Paul had it all together until we had dinner with him and Shirley, and I saw him belittle her all evening. I have now decided that the only perfect people in the world are those we keep at a safe distance.

You might as well confess it: Your wife occasionally gets

depressed; your husband has no affinity for yard work; your kids have little interest in pushing in their dresser drawers; your preacher is no great shakes as an orator; and your best friend has been known to embellish the truth. We will live and die surrounded by imperfect people. To wait for the perfect "anybody" to walk into our lives is to wait for a world we will never have.

A friend echoed these too-high expectations when he dropped by the office recently to sip coffee and discuss recent church events. "I'm disappointed," he complained, "in the way some people in our church have behaved, people I thought were truly spiritual. I had them on pedestals, and it's been hard to see them as so unspiritual in these matters. People I thought were really close to God have been mean and unforgiving."

I know his disappointment because I too have felt it. But then, nobody belongs on a pedestal. *We* are to blame for elevating ordinary people into realms where only the Divine belongs. Worse, we set ourselves up for disillusionment.

How do we handle others' imperfections? We accept them, laugh at them, joke about them, pray for personal tolerance. Of course, there are boundaries to every imperfection; sometimes we must act decisively. If your spouse batters you, call the police and pack your suitcase. If the kids get too wild, assume strong parental authority and lay down the law. If the senator is "on the take," oust him. Generally speaking, though, we need to be more tolerant, more forgiving, more willing to love people as they are. The problem in our world is not a lack of justice, it is a lack of grace.

Making People in My Image

One natural response to someone's imperfection is to take that person on as a reclamation project. We see so clearly the speck in our brother's eye and feel it is our God-given duty to remove it. Sadly, one false ideal gives birth to another: Our need for perfect people leads to a need to change people.

A fifth "great expectation" that sends many of us into misery is this idea that we *can* change others. We spend much of our lives in frustration because these imperfect people around us seem impervious to our agenda for their lives. They are totally blind to our astonishing wisdom and stay stuck in their flaws.

Anyone who has read the Bible knows that we are to be creative agents of change in the world. We are to be salt, light, ambassadors, reconcilers, and witnesses. God has given us a mandate to make a positive difference in society, and we cannot take that mandate lightly.

That does not mean, however, that we can change anybody. At best, we might be able to help someone who already wants to change. The motivation for personal transformation, though, is always internal. Any time *we* propose the change, plan the program, and provide the initiative, the reclamation project is doomed from the start.

I have personally taken under wing several people whose lives obviously needed a major overhaul. I entered the reformation business with great confidence, certain that my shining example and profound words of counsel would work miracles. In my mind, I saw ugly caterpillars transforming into glorious butterflies because of my influence.

Alas, it was not to be. The caterpillars stayed caterpillars. My best efforts brought forth no butterflies. The reason for the failure, I see now, was that the transformation was *my* idea, *my* project. The caterpillars were quite content, thank you, with what they were. They had no desire to work, study, save money, seek forgiveness, or do any of the other difficult things that would make the transformation possible. I have learned the hard way that personal change without personal motivation is impossible.

The dark side of this interaction is the frustration we

agents of change put ourselves through. It is not fun to watch people, especially people we love, wallow in self-induced agony. We feel a great need to *do* something, to effect change whether they want it or not. Is there anything more exasperating than seeing a vision of promise for someone who cannot see it himself?

But there is a bright side, too. Our inability to change people insures that not everybody will be like us. When we draw up agendas and plan personalities, we begin to make others in our own image. We want them to think like us, relate to people the way we do, see life as we do. If those poor caterpillars in our care ever do sprout wings, their spots will be identical to ours.

Do we really qualify as models of perfection? Is it possible that someone else's vision of his life is more accurate than our vision of his life? Our inability to "pull the strings" for others reminds us that we are not God after all.

Though we would like to have God's power, we don't. We can love others, encourage them to be different, and then do all we can to assist them if *they* decide to change. For ultimately, change comes from within. Until we recognize that, we "changers" are creating unnecessary stress in our own lives. None of us can stand up under the strain of being God for someone else.

Only a Primer

The five ideas I've mentioned in this chapter are but a grain of sand on the beach of false expectations. If one were to write about all of the mistaken notions by which we live, there would not be enough paper in the world to hold the words.

I hope this chapter can be a primer, a beginning place that can at least prompt us to look again at our life maps. And, in particular, to make five affirmations that can help us build a truthful life:

• As intelligent, witty, and loving as I am, not everyone

will like me. I will be true to my self anyway, and remember that the only perfect person who ever walked the face of the earth got crucified.

• I will never completely escape struggle, and I will inevitably spend some time in the jaws of the dragon. I will not curse either God or myself when life gets difficult.

• God will never be as understandable as I would like. But I will remember that if someone like me could comprehend God, He wouldn't *be* God. I will thank Him that He is bigger than any bottle I will ever try to put Him in.

• I will quit criticizing the people in my world for their imperfections and start accepting them as they are. I will quit looking for perfect people and be grateful for the flawed, ordinary ones God has given me.

• I will give up the idea of changing the world and leave that to God. I will try to change *myself* first, and then be available to others who genuinely want to change.

Those five affirmations can remind us that some of our other long-held, deeply-entrenched, almost-sacred ideas and habits need to be examined. Tragically, some of the lines we've etched on our maps are leading us miles away from the abundant life that is supposed to be ours.

If you remember nothing else from this chapter, hold on to this one truth: Only a fool keeps following a map that leads to misery.

For Reflection and Discussion

1. Do you ever put on a false face to win approval? How much of your stress comes from trying to be something you're not?

2. Do you ever dream of a life free of struggle? Do you ever blame God when things don't go your way?

3. Have you ever had God in a bottle? As you have matured as a Christian, has God gotten more mysterious or less? Does it ever frustrate you that God does not give more explicit answers to life's problems?

4. Are there certain people you expect to be perfect? Are you overly critical of some of those close to you?

5. Have you ever taken on someone as a reclamation project? Do you ever get discouraged because people won't change?

6. How long has it been since you examined your life map? Do you have some other false expectations that need to be corrected?

7. List below some specific changes you must make to update your map and move toward joyful living:
   1.
   2.
   3.
   4.

Woe to you, teachers of the law and Pharisees, you hypocrites! You are like whitewashed tombs, which look beautiful on the outside but on the inside are full of dead men's bones and everything unclean.

Matthew 23:27

"The church, as I have known it, has been pretty much the congregation of the unblessed. Perhaps that is why I love it; I harbor so much unblessedness in myself, and the good people who try harder to be better and better are my sisters and brothers."

Karl Olsson, *Come to the Party*

9

PERFECTLY MISERABLE

I would like to think that *anyone* would profit from the ideas in this book, but my words are really aimed at people like myself—people who claim Jesus as their Lord, the Bible as their book, and the church as their community.

In this chapter, I want to address a type of stress that is primarily an evangelical phenomenon. It is an anxiety reserved for those of us who sincerely desire to be "good Christians." It is the stress of pious pretense, that distorted, overblown attempt to look "spiritual" that ends up draining us of joy. There is nothing more tiring than trying to hold up a perpetual mask of perfection, nothing more burdensome than trying to carry the ponderous law of righteousness on our feeble shoulders.

In reflecting on my own spiritual journey and in observing hundreds of fine Christians through the years, I'm convinced many of us are worn out and run down from trying to appear better than we really are. The mantle of divinity does not rest comfortably upon us, but every day we slip it on and gamely smile through its scratchy irritation.

The Balancing Act

No one ever said being a Christian was easy. True, most of us today don't face cruel persecution like some of our ancestors did, but we have our battles to fight nonetheless. Most of these battles are inner ones, waged in the dark recesses of our soul. And the outcome of these private tussles determines the extent of our joy and the quality of our witness.

The Christian life is hard because, lived well, it is a fine balance. Think of all the tensions we Christians feel, all of the pulls on our faith. There is the tension, for example, between grace and works; between saving the world and savoring it; between private piety and public involvement; between a healthy passion and an unhealthy fanaticism; between our will and God's will and how we discern the difference. I think the best symbol for the contemporary Christian might well be a tight-rope walker carefully traversing a high wire. If he leans too far in either direction, he falls headlong into trouble. Only the net of God's grace prevents disaster.

The tension I'm asking you to face is the tension between too much worldliness and too much religion—the age-old battle of being *in* the world, but not *of* it. If we fall on the side of worldliness, our salt loses its savor and our light is snuffed under a bushel. If we fall on the side of religion, we become sweet, syrupy Christians out of touch with the real world. Blessed (and rare!) is the man or woman who can live in the world, even love the world, and still be true to Christ.

Most of the time we feel caught between the "Christian world" and the "secular world." We feel we must choose between the two worlds, and no matter which way we go, we lose something. Thomas Howard, in his book, *Christ the*

Tiger, saw his choice like this: "I felt that I was in a limbo, with, on the one hand, a familiar world of orthodoxy in which I could no longer breathe, and, on the other, 'the world,' which posed a threat to my purity and my pursuit of authenticity."

You see? Heads, you lose. Tails, you lose.

What we must always strive for is that delicate balance between the two worlds. Or, maybe better said, a radical embracing of both worlds. Howard found a flesh-and-blood model of one who loved both God and life:

> He worried me because he loved both God and life at the same time. It had always been one or the other for me. When I had tried to pursue God, I had fled from life. When life began to be dazzling, I had let God slip. I would have called his voluptuous zest for life pagan except that it was not only matched by his appetite for God: it was part of it. . . . I was jarred to discover that my friend had no dichotomy in his mind between spiritual things and other things. One was to love the world and experience because God did and because one loved God. How else is one to express joy and worship but in merriment and affirmation? Joy was an important part of his creed.

There are two key words in that last sentence: "creed" and "joy." To be biblical people we must have a creed, a framework of faith, a set of convictions. But to be biblical people we must also have joy. We must know that God wants us joyful and that when Christ said He came to give abundant life, He wasn't just mouthing a cliché.

Are you heavy on creed and light on joy? Have you fallen so much in the direction of piety that you have lost touch with your humanity? It is time to embrace life and slide free from the awful burden of religion.

How to Be a Pharisee and Not Even Know It

The Pharisees were masters of pious pretense. It's rather ironic, really. The Pharisees were at the synagogue every time the doors opened, studied Scripture exhaustively and served as models of the circumspect life. Yet Jesus directed His fiercest anger toward them. When we read a passage like Matthew 23, where Jesus hurls a barrage of "woes" at these religious leaders, the fire of His wrath is searing.

Over and over Jesus described these men as "hypocrites." The Greek word *hupokrites* was the word used in the ancient world for an actor. Jesus saw these men as mask-wearers and pretenders who were playing a dangerous game called "Impressive Religion."

A Pharisee, ancient or modern, is marked by four characteristics:

1. *A Pharisee plays to the crowd.* Jesus put it this way:

> Everything they do is done for men to see: They make their phylacteries wide and the tassels of their prayer shawls long; they love the place of honor at banquets and the most important seats in the synagogues; they love to be greeted in the marketplaces and to have men call them 'Rabbi' (Matt. 23:5–7).

Pharisees, in other words, have an exaggerated interest in reputation. When they visit the sick, or make a generous offering to the church, or read the Bible through in a year, they make sure that someone notices and applauds their devotion. Jesus, on the other hand, advocated a faith that shuns any semblance of showiness. Giving, He said, is to be done in secret. Prayer is to be offered in the closet. Fasting is to be accomplished without anyone knowing about it. Here is one of the fundamental differences between the Pharisees and Jesus: The Pharisees played before an audience of thousands; Jesus played before an audience of One.

2. *A Pharisee is blind to his own sin.* Pharisees are expert at seeing the awful sins of the world. They chide criminals, secular humanists and pornographers with vengeance. They are not so adept, unfortunately, at detecting the sin in their own lives.

> Woe to you, teachers of the law and Pharisees, you
> hypocrites! You clean the outside of the cup and dish,
> but inside they are full of greed and self-indulgence.
> Blind Pharisee! First clean the inside of the cup and dish,
> and then the outside will also be clean (Matt. 23:25–26).

Make no mistake, the outside of the cup does shine
impressively. These are moral, church-going people. But
their sin is the most ironic: the sin of not knowing they are
sinners.

3. *A Pharisee emphasizes rules over people.*

> Woe to you, teachers of the law and Pharisees, you
> hypocrites! You give a tenth of your spices—mint, dill,
> and cummin. But you have neglected the more important
> matters of the law—justice, mercy, and faithfulness. You
> should have practiced the latter, without neglecting the
> former. You blind guides! You strain out a gnat but swal-
> low a camel (Matt. 23:23–24).

Pharisees are rule-keepers, which, in itself, is admira-
ble. In a civil society, rules are for keeping, not breaking.
But rule keeping, with just a slight twist, becomes legalism,
and legalism will absolutely destroy everything Jesus stood
for. Legalism tithes mint, dill and cummin, and forgets
justice, mercy and faithfulness. It draws up intricate
church by-laws and neglects ministry. It builds gigantic
buildings and overlooks hungry people. It carefully follows
Robert's Rules of Order and omits common sense. Legalism
even observes protocol and kills a carpenter.

4. *A Pharisee makes religion an obligation, not a blessing.*
Hear Jesus again:

> They tie up heavy loads and put them on men's shoul-
> ders, but they themselves are not willing to lift a finger
> to move them (Matt. 23:4).

Modern Pharisees load people down with "ought's" and
"should's." They make the dance of eternal life a laborious
trudge. Naturally, this approach to God turns the world
away in droves:

119

> Woe to you, teachers of the law and Pharisees, you hypocrites! You shut the kingdom of heaven in men's faces (Matt. 23:13).

Even when it does win converts, pharisaic spirituality only enslaves:

> Woe to you, teachers of the law and Pharisees, you hypocrites! You travel over land and sea to win a single convert, and when he becomes one, you make him twice as much a son of hell as you are (Matt. 23:15).

There is just no joy, no life in the Pharisees' religion, and you can always spot a member of the "godly" sect by the somber, "spiritual" look on his face.

These four tragic flaws are spooky because Jesus found them in such upright people. I tremble when I read Matthew 23, that shocking passage that uncovers these spiritual defects in religious people. I tremble because I know how easily we "good Christians" can slip into this kind of religion. And I also know that this brand of spirituality is as reprehensible to Christ now as it was then.

But trembling can be a prelude to discovering, so let's use Matthew 23 to discover again who we are supposed to be:

We are the people who live before an audience of One.

We are the people who readily admit our sin and then splash in God's abundant forgiveness.

We are the people who know that love always takes precedence over rules.

We are the people who have been set free to live with joyous abandon.

Honesty Is the Only Policy

What the Pharisees needed, and what we need, is a good dose of honesty. We need to remove the mask, cut the pretense and be real. Only when we are honest with

120

God and honest with men will our faith mean anything to us.

Annie Dillard writes, "I get in my little canoe and paddle out to the edge of mystery. . . . Every single thing I follow takes me there, to the edge of a cliff. As soon as I start writing, I'm hanging over the cliff again. You can make a perfectly coherent world at the snap of a finger—but only if you don't bother being honest about it." The Christian must always *bother* to be honest about it, to live the truth in relationship to God and to man. Being honest about it is the only cure for pious pretense.

First, we have to be honest with God. Our prayers cannot be mechanical cliches. We cannot traffic in trivia and expect to build a faith that is worth anything. We must bare our soul before the One who created us. He knows us anyway, so why play games? We must speak to Him of our doubts, fears, disappointments and ecstasies. Like Job, we may find ourselves at times questioning God or complaining to Him. Thankfully, He is big enough to hear our confusion, and even indignation, and still love us. I think He would rather hear us honestly moan, or even scream, than to hear a grown-up version of "Now I lay me down to sleep. . . ."

Then, we must be honest with people. At least with some people, the mask must come down. We have to confess our humanity. The only hope we have for joy and witness is to be real with people, to tell how it is in our heart. The saddest thing about pharisaic spirituality is its devastating result: It douses the joy and destroys credibility with ordinary people. Who among us enjoys relating to "pedestal people," people with easy answers, impeccable credentials and painted smiles? What we need are regular human beings to love us. And that is precisely what we need to be for those around us.

Removing the Veil

Many of us can readily identify with the dilemma Moses faced in Exodus 34. After he came down from his encounter with God on Mount Sinai, his face shone with the radiance of the Lord. His time alone with God gave him a countenance that literally glowed. Consequently, he was then viewed with awe by the Israelites. Unfortunately, he then faced a new pressure.

The Apostle Paul, in commenting on Moses' experience, tells us that he put a veil over his face "to keep the Israelites from gazing at it while the radiance was fading away" (2 Cor. 3:13). What a predicament for a Christian leader! The glow is gone. The splendor has faded. The face is that of an ordinary human. And the people will be terribly disappointed if he shows up in public without his customary radiance.

What do *we* do when faced with such a predicament? Exactly what Moses did—we put on a veil, pretend perfection, and mask our humanity with piety. We put up a spiritual facade.

Paul tells us to go ahead and remove the veil and let our real face show. "We are not like Moses, who would put a veil over his face" (2 Cor. 3:13). He tells us, in fact, that it is in showing our real face to the world that God can use us: "And we, who with unveiled faces all reflect the Lord's glory, are being transformed into his likeness with ever-increasing glory, which comes from the Lord, who is the Spirit" (2 Cor. 3:18).

Two things stand out about that statement. First, Paul seems to be saying that only unveiled faces can reflect God's glory. God has a strange affinity for ordinary faces! As long as Moses had a radiant face or a veiled face, the people revered him, and looked up to him as one who had a unique relationship with God. One thing they would not do, however, is identify with him and see him as a fellow human being. People with radiant faces always seem special and unapproachable.

Moses, take off the veil. Be real before God and the people. It's the only way God can really use you to reflect His glory. As long as the veil is in place, you will be admired.

But only when the veil comes off can you be truly loved.

The second thing Paul says is that only unveiled faces can be transformed. Our unveiled faces "are being transformed into his likeness." Why, in the name of common sense, would people with a heavenly radiance, people with a perpetual spiritual glow need to change? Well, they wouldn't. Only the sick pray for healing, only the blind yearn for sight, and only those with ordinary faces long for transformation. A basic prerequisite for change is the knowledge that we don't always glow, that our face is often quite plain and even homely. God can transform us only when we confess that we need to be transformed.

Moses, take off the veil—and vow never to put it on again. It's the only way God can begin to change you and make you more like Him. As long as the veil is in place, you will have a fine reputation among the brethren. But only when the veil comes off can you have honest, transforming relationships.

Paying for Pretense

Where do we go to get training in such honesty? Is there a place where we can learn to remove the veil and be honest before God and people? The obvious answer, of course, is the church. We get training in the "truth that sets us free" from the community of faith.

Sadly, that answer can be erroneous. In fact, the church can even lead us away from the freedom of honesty. Eugene Peterson says, in *Traveling Light*:

> The gravest threats to the free life do not come from the atheist or the secularist. They come from the quarter we might least suspect—from religion, particularly a former religion, a childhood religion, a neurotic religion. Living in the free air of freedom with its insecurities and chilling breezes, we are subject to sudden nostalgia for the warm, secure swaddling clothes of an earlier religion, inconspicuous compromises with the environment: an

Egyptian calf-god, a Judaistic circumcision, sentimental-
ized prayers, stereotyped emotions, formula explana-
tions.

When the church offers us these things, it cannot help
us shed pious pretense. We must make our private vow to
be honest with God and people, and then pray daily for
the wisdom and courage to keep that vow. It will free us
from the exacting price of pretense.

What toll does pious pretense exact?

It costs us an awareness of God's forgiveness. As long
as we're sinless and perfect, why do we need "amazing
grace"? Only those who have glimpsed the reality of their
own sin can sing that song with gusto.

It costs us intimacy with others. Pretense stiff-arms people. It erects barricades that block people out. Do you really
think common people rushed to Pharisees to talk sports or
celebrate a job promotion?

It costs us inner peace. Because we are detached from
God's forgiveness, because we have few close relationships,
and because somewhere deep within us we know our goodness is a facade, we live with constant anxiety. Nothing is
more stressful than trying to bluff our way through life.

Authentic Faith

Exaggerate godly virtues ever so slightly and we wind
up with that style of religion Jesus so clearly detested. What
we want is *authentic* faith. Each of us must take our Bible,
experiences and heritage and try to fashion such a faith.

For me, several facets of authentic faith have gradually
come into focus.

Authentic faith has both conviction and joy.

Authentic faith can live with the tension of paradox. It
doesn't have to see everything as black or white, neatly
defined in little boxes.

Authentic faith is not afraid to ask questions and dig
for truth.

Authentic faith is honest. It doesn't babble platitudes and drown itself in religious jargon.

Authentic faith is built around "the great commandment." It makes love for God and others its top priority.

Authentic faith is dynamic. It changes and deepens through the passages of life.

Authentic faith is centered on the cross. It understands the breathtaking implications—freedom, grace, eternal celebration—of Jesus' death. Authentic faith gives peace.

Because it goes to the core of our being, authentic faith gives us a solid foundation upon which to build our lives. If we build on the shifting sand of slick church programs, fleeting spiritual fads and clever three-point sermons, we'll never stand when the winds begin to howl.

If, on the other hand, we build on the bedrock of truth, we'll survive even when accosted by a whirlwind. And, knowing that our foundation is solid, we will be able to live at peace.

For Reflection and Discussion

1. Do you detect much pious pretense in the contemporary church? Do you think pious pretense hurts the church's witness?

2. Do you ever feel as if you live in two worlds—a secular world and a religious one? Are you a different person in each world?

3. Which of the four tragic flaws in the Pharisees' brand of spirituality is most evident in your life?

4. Do you identify with Moses' struggle to hide his face? Do you have any people before whom you can remove the veil?

5. Is your church a place where people can remove the veil and be honest before God and others? What can you do to make your church more loving?

6. Think about your own relationships. Do you enjoy being around "pedestal people"? Or do you gravitate toward those whose humanity is showing?

7. What for you are the five most important characteristics of authentic faith?
   1.
   2.
   3.
   4.
   5.

8. Are you living by the creed outlined in those five characteristics?

Where sin increased, grace increased all the more.

Romans 5:20

"It is about as hard to absolve yourself of your own guilt as it is to sit in your own lap."

Frederick Buechner, *Wishful Thinking*

10

CHAINED TO YESTERDAY

*T*he gun is up. The marathoners lean expectantly at the starting line, waiting for the *bang* that will propel them on a twenty-six-mile journey of exhilarating exhaustion.

They are, to a man, thin, almost gaunt. Their miles of training through the years have pared all the fat off their bones. They are sleek and hawk-like, built for gliding through the countryside.

All are dressed in the usual marathoner's attire—flimsy T-shirt, scanty shorts, lightweight running shoes. They all know that the less weight they carry the better their chance for victory.

All but one, that is. Perched in the back of the pack at the starting line is one comical figure who looks shockingly out of place. This runner is wearing a heavy topcoat, ear muffs and rain galoshes. In each hand he carries a large suitcase, which judging by the stoop in his shoulders, are loaded with something heavy.

The gun sounds, and the runners leap off the starting line like greyhounds after a jack rabbit. All but the comical figure in the rear of the pack, who can only trudge down the road. He is so encumbered with clothing and suitcases it is impossible for him to keep pace with the other runners. As the race begins, the spectators don't know who will win. They do know, however, who will lose. Unless the man in the overcoat sheds his burdens, he doesn't stand a chance. For him, it will be a long, long run.

A Woeful Look at Some Weary Saints

The absurdity of anyone trying to run a marathon with such a ponderous load is bizarre, not funny. That imaginary marathoner represents all of us who live loaded down with guilt. He is a picture of all who try to maintain a loving marriage, raise children, work at a job, serve in the church, and find life a joy while burdened with the heavy baggage of past sin. And if that runner symbolizes you, then you are in for a long, long run.

Eventually, you will find yourself under too much stress to continue the race. You will conclude that running is just too hard, and will have to choose among other options— grimly walking to the finish line, taking frequent and long rest stops, breaking down and spending time in the hospital, or just quitting the race altogether.

I think it would be interesting to have a guilt detector at the entrance of our church—something along the lines of the security detectors used at airports. When a person enters the door, guilt is immediately detected and a buzzer sounds. That individual then has to unload his guilt or he cannot leave the sanctuary! Wouldn't it be wonderful if church was the place we could drop our burdens? Wouldn't it be great if we could go to church not to be scolded, but to be forgiven? And wouldn't we all be more joyful if we could get out from under the crushing load of our guilt?

One would think that Christians would be experts at dumping guilt and living with freedom. Christians, after all, know a gospel of grace, forgiveness and reconciliation. Don't we?

Unfortunately, the smiling, contented people who traipse into the sanctuary on Sunday morning bring with them an unbelievable amount of guilt. Even worse, those same people usually leave the sanctuary as miserable as they entered it. Many, in truth, will leave feeling *guiltier.* After all, don't all of these other Christians have it all together? And isn't the preacher prescribing a godliness one can never attain?

Sorting Through the Guilt Pile

Our guilt comes from a dizzying variety of directions. Were we to pile it at the church's front door, we would find a surprising array of hurts, regrets and sins. If we took the time to sort through the pile, we would find:

- the failed marriage, begun in hope and the passion of romance, ended in the ashes of disillusionment, depression and anger.
- the less-than-ideal children, not at all what the parents envisioned when they brought them into the world.
- the affair, conceived in lust and consummated in secrecy.
- the alcoholism, perhaps even now denied as a problem.
- the successful career, which has made a man both wealthy and alienated from everyone he's supposed to love.
- the church spat, forgotten history to all but the one who cannot forget her part in it.
- the lustful thoughts that will not go away, filling the man with gratitude that no one can read his mind.
- the aged parents, pining away in the nursing home while the guilt-ridden children climb the ladder of success.
- the "tremendous potential," long proclaimed by

family and friends but not yet fulfilled.
- the trumped up spirituality that smiles and looks real but is disgustingly empty.
- the vague, undefinable feeling that we have somehow failed God when all we wanted to do was love Him.

Those are just a few of the *big* guilts in the pile. Closer scrutiny reveals a bunch of *little* guilts, too—yesterday's marital tiff, unjustifiably barking at the kids, neglecting to visit an acquaintance in the hospital, the lingering look at the lingerie ad, skipping church to watch a ball game.

The Apostle Paul once said that he had to forget those things which were behind him (Phil. 3:13). No doubt, he would have been a miserable creature if he had lugged his past sins with him on his missionary tours. We may not have his particular sins—consenting to Stephen's death, persecuting Christians, legalism and whatever others he had—but we have plenty of our own to toss onto the pile. The buzzer on our guilt detector had better be powered by strong batteries, for it will be sounding almost continuously! And if we cannot forget those things behind us, we are destined for misery.

Guilt—Friend or Foe?

At first brush, guilt seems to be a sinister thing. Can something that inflicts so much pain on the human race be anything but sinister?

Some psychology experts loudly trumpet the uselessness and destructiveness of guilt. Wayne Dyer, in *Your Erroneous Zones*, says:

> Guilt is the most useless of all erroneous zone behaviors. It is by far the greatest waste of emotional energy. Why? Because, by definition, you are feeling immobilized in the present over something that has *already* taken place, and no amount of guilt can ever change history.

Since guilt is so demonic, the only logical thing to do,

the experts contend, is change our attitude about those things that cause it. Dyer continues:

> You can begin to change your attitude about the things over which you experience guilt. Our culture has many strains of puritanical thinking which send messages like, "If it's fun, you're supposed to feel guilty about it." Many of your own self-inflicted guilt reactions can be traced to this kind of thinking. Perhaps you've learned that you shouldn't indulge yourself, or you mustn't enjoy a dirty joke, or you ought not to participate in a certain kind of sexual behavior. While the restraining messages are omnipresent in our culture, guilt about enjoying yourself is purely self-inflicted.

This approach begins with the premise that guilt is a useless emotion. Therefore, we must change our thinking about those activities that are making us feel guilty. The activities aren't wrong; our guilt feelings about them are.

This popular approach to guilt is right in many ways. Lingering guilt *is* destructive. We *do* need to change our thinking about some harmless actions that provoke our guilt feelings. Much guilt *is* useless and teaches us nothing. Guilt *can't* change history. Those truths are worth knowing, and the popular concept reminds us of them.

But this philosophy of guilt has one major drawback: It fails to differentiate between legitimate guilt and illegitimate guilt. It lumps all remorse into one bundle labeled "guilt," when in truth there should be two bundles: remorse that is legitimate because it stems from sin, and remorse that is illegitimate because it stems from neurosis.

Some of our guilt is false and can cause tragic neurosis. That kind needs to be rejected. But some of our guilt is a nudge from God. Stephen Brown reminds us in *No More Mr. Nice Guy*:

> One of the most dangerous practices in which some people engage is the practice of denying the legitimate feeling of guilt. When I have violated God's standards (or, for that matter, my own best standards), I ought to

feel guilty. Unless I accurately identify what the feeling of unease is, I will not be able to do anything about alleviating the unease. A sense of guilt in the face of the violation of legitimate standards is legitimate guilt.

Guilt does not have to be useless and destructive. Illegitimate guilt always is, but legitimate guilt can be useful and constructive. If we know how to deal with it, our guilt can be a friend instead of a foe. As Thomas Oden writes in his book, *Guilt Free*, "It is time to recognize that guilt has something to do with the way God is drawing us quietly toward the purpose of our existence."

A Call to a Better Self

One of the fine things our guilt does for us is call us to a better self. It serves as a prod that motivates us to change.

Oden uses an analogy that is helpful in understanding this benefit of legitimate guilt. He likens running a life to running a democratic government. Each, he asserts, has three branches with specific responsibilities.

First, there is the legislative branch. In government, this branch makes laws. It looks to the future and constructs a legal framework that will help make society safe and just. In the human life, the legislative branch allows us to dream dreams, make investments and consider future possibilities. It looks ahead and makes plans. Hope comes from this legislative branch of our lives.

Second, there is the executive branch. In government, this branch implements legislative plans and carries out the proposed action. In life, our executive branch concerns itself with the present. It carries out hope's orders and tells us what to do today—what to wear, how to treat our children, which car to buy. The executive branch is practical and thrives on doing. Action comes from this branch of our lives.

Third, there is the judicial branch. The judicial branch of government judges, makes assessments and determines consequences. It tries cases and issues rewards and punishments. In the human life, the corresponding judicial branch enables us to evaluate ourselves, to look behind us and see the tracks we've made. Conscience is a part of the judicial branch; it tells us what we *ought* to have been and done. Both the sweet taste of nostalgia and the sharp jab of guilt come from this third branch of our lives.

My point is that all three branches are indispensable. Remove any one from either a government or an individual life and things fall to pieces. We must tend to future, present *and* past. Planning, implementing and evaluating are necessary functions of any good government—or any good life.

Guilt, then, is sometimes a friend. Guilt arises out of the judicial caucuses of our brain to remind us that we have not been what we should have been. It is the scale that measures the discrepancy between the actual and the ideal. If we eradicate all legitimate guilt from our minds, we've lost the pain that prompts us to change. We've shut down the judicial branch that allows us to assess our lives and respond accordingly.

Legitimate guilt is like fever. It signals us that something is wrong internally, that an infection called sin is loose in our soul. And, like fever, guilt is a gift that warns us that something must be done if we are to be healed. Nobody in his right mind enjoys running a high fever, but it is far worse to let infection run wild without any warning. So, too, nobody wants to feel the pain of guilt. But it is a much worse fate to move away from God's will and not even know it.

The Greek word for sin in the New Testament literally means "to miss the mark." God has a bull's-eye for each life, a target of love, peace and productivity that we are to hit. When we fire our arrows, joy is the result of good aim; guilt is the result of misfires. But can we honestly say that guilt is sinister when it is prodding us to be better marksmen, when it is issuing a loud, albeit painful, call to a better self?

I think about David's awful guilt in Psalm 51. After his adulterous escapade with Bathsheba, the prophet Nathan confronted him with his sin. David immediately felt guilty (legitimate guilt, I might add, stemming from terrible wrongdoing) and confessed it in the psalm:

> Have mercy on me, O God, according to your un-failing love; according to your great compassion blot out my transgressions. Wash all my iniquity and cleanse me from my sin. For I know my transgressions, and my sin is always before me. Against you, you only, have I sinned and done what is evil in your sight . . . (Ps. 51:1–4).

Shall we encourage David to quit wallowing in his misery? Shall we tell him his guilt is just a psychological hang-up, a waste of emotional energy that should be directed elsewhere? I think not. His guilt was a good friend, searing his conscience with the branding iron of remorse, leading him to repentance. The friend did David a favor; it called him to restring the bow, take aim again at the bull's-eye, and fire another arrow. His guilt called him to a better self.

A Call to the Cross

I have supposedly learned how to be my own best friend, eliminated my erroneous zones, gotten in touch with my feelings, taken steps toward self-actualization, tried to liberate the "child" within me, and been told that I'm okay and you're okay. My problem is: In spite of my best efforts, I know deep-down that I'm *not* okay, nor am I too sure about you. There is a mean, selfish tiger within me that refuses to be tamed.

I have tried most of the prescribed religious medicines to tranquilize him. I have attended church, read Scripture, prayed, witnessed to my friends, discussed theology with kindred spirits, attended seminars, read hundreds of religious books, confessed sin, walked aisles, preached sermons and affected an air of righteous piety. The results have been less than encouraging. I still find myself stuck in sin. Despite my finest efforts, I am still selfish, lustful, proud, indifferent and a host of other unsavory qualities too numerous to mention.

My response to my shortcomings is like David's in Psalm 51: I feel guilty. On my more honest days, I even admit that I'll never measure up, that I'll never get it all together, that the biblical ideal will always elude me. I am forced to conclude that without a Rescuer I am doomed—which is the second thing that guilt does for us. Not only does our guilt call us to a better self, it also calls us to the cross and makes us gasp in wonder at the gift of love Christ gave us there. Guilt is our friend because it sends us running to Jesus.

As we saw in the last chapter, Jesus tried to get the Pharisees to feel some guilt, because without it they would never find salvation. A respectable, upright, religious leader simply sees no need for a Savior. An honest, struggling, ordinary sinner will grab on to one like a starving man who suddenly finds bread—an analogy Jesus himself used when He proclaimed himself the eternal Bread of life. Guilt is that desperate hunger that leads us to the Bread.

One Pharisee who did eventually feast on the Bread was the Apostle Paul, but even after his conversion he struggled with his sin and guilt. In Romans 7, he wrestled with the ambiguity in his soul and declared himself a wretched man. But an awareness of his sinfulness and Christ's victory over it, enabled him to sing, "Therefore, there is now no condemnation for those who are in Christ Jesus . . ." (Rom. 8:1). His guilt pushed him, not to the brink of despair, but to the gates of grace.

Paul knew that when Jesus died, the door of the prison was flung open. No one need live under the curse of guilt anymore. Anyone desperate enough to leave the security of the cell can walk out a free person and begin to revel in God's grace. Whosoever will may come.

God in Christ opened the door once and for all. It is still up to each of us as individuals, though, to step out into the sunshine. Our salvation is not completed until we accept the freedom Christ died to purchase. Is there a sadder picture anywhere than the one depicting a prisoner sagging in the corner of a dark jail house while the door to glorious freedom stands wide open?

Guilt is our ally because it moves us toward the door. When we, like Paul, realize that on our own we cannot conquer our sin, when we finally see that all of our attempts to escape the prison by sawing on window bars with the fingernail file of morality are in vain, when we at last admit that we're *not* okay, that something *is* fundamentally wrong with us—then and only then are we ready to fall before the cross and claim its gift.

Suspicious of God's Sales Pitch

Quite often, I receive notification that I have been selected to receive a fabulous prize. I must be the luckiest man on the face of the earth! The smooth-talking gentleman on the phone tells me that I am the grand prize winner, and that if I will cooperate and take just a brief tour of his company's gorgeous lake resort I can claim my prize. Or the notice comes in the mail that I have been chosen to receive a television, a Lincoln Continental, or a $10,000 check if only I will enroll in this club or subscribe to this magazine. Invariably, I give the salesman a short (but polite!) rebuff, or I toss the come-on envelope into the trash can.

Why? Because I've learned that nothing is free. At one time, I ran to the lake resort to claim my car, clock and cash, only to return home exhausted and angered with a couple of cheap trinkets to show for my efforts. Now I am wiser and more suspicious. Like most of America, I have become more astute about grandiose promises.

Fortunately, God is infinitely more trustworthy than modern advertisers. When He says "we are justified freely by his grace through the redemption that came by Jesus

Christ" (Rom. 3:24), we can believe it. When He says "there is no more condemnation for those who are in Christ Jesus" (Rom. 8:1), He really means it. When He tells us to "rejoice in God through our Lord Jesus Christ, through whom we have now received the reconciliation" (Rom. 5:11), I think it is quite appropriate to kill the fatted calf and begin to make merry.

Ah, but trained cynics that we are, we will not believe it. Nothing that wonderful could be ours simply by faith, simply by believing it is so and living accordingly. Sure God forgives sin—but not *my* particular, terrible sin. Not *my* divorce, or *my* affair, or *my* alcoholism, or *my* pride, or *my* lack of spiritual fervor. When we get the call that tells us of free forgiveness, we don't exactly hang up on God, but neither do we dance for joy or weep tears of gratitude.

It is time to believe God's offer. It is time to leave the guilty past behind and get on with the race that still must be run.

Free to Run

I have a hope. My hope is that ordinary people will begin to listen to their guilt and hear its paradoxical message: (1) You can change and be more tomorrow than you are today, and (2) You are loved and valued by God just as you are. Those are the two sides of the Christian street— commitment and grace—and guilt can lead us to both.

Somewhere, midway through the race, a miraculous transformation takes place. The marathoner drops his luggage, sheds his heavy clothing and begins to travel light. Without the extra weight, he is a surprisingly swift runner. He settles into a smooth stride, begins to wave at spectators, smells the flowers and feels the breeze in his face.

For him, a whole new race has begun.

For Reflection and Discussion

1. Do you identify with the burdened runner in this chapter? What specific past sins and experiences are weighing you down?

2. Do you agree that guilt can be either legitimate or illegitimate? If so, how would you differentiate between the two?

3. Has guilt ever called you to a better self? Have you ever made some specific changes in your life because you experienced guilt?

4. Have you ever tried "religious medicine" to relieve your guilt? Did it work?

5. Think about the "I'm okay, you're okay" philosophy. Do you agree or disagree with it? Do you find it compatible with the gospel?

6. Do you ever have trouble believing the Good News is as good as it is? Have you personally accepted the truth that the prison door is open and God wants you forgiven and free? What is keeping you from living in the freedom Christ died to give you?

7. Is your guilt pushing you toward deeper commitment? Or a deeper appreciation of grace? Or both?

Therefore, I urge you, brothers, in view of God's mercy, to offer your bodies as living sacrifices, holy and pleasing to God—which is your spiritual worship.

Romans 12:1

"No one ever told us that the body determined our mental and spiritual energies. That with the new body we can put on the new person and build a new life, the life we were always designed to lead but lost with the body we enjoyed in our youth."

George Sheehan, *Running and Being*

11

THE GNOSTIC TRAP

*W*hen I was a fledgling preacher, long on passion and short on wisdom, I had one illustration I used repeatedly. It was one of those all-purpose illustrations that could be smuggled into nearly any sermon, so I used it with monotonous regularity. The illustration was supposed to reveal how we humans focus on the "physical" to the neglect of the "spiritual."

"Just imagine," I would say with as much authority as I could muster, "that a man is given a present by one of his friends. The present is neatly wrapped in a small box with a pretty bow on top. Imagine that the man opens the box and discovers a huge diamond inside. He is flabbergasted at his friend's extravagance, and thanks him effusively. But then the man takes the gift home, removes the diamond from the box, and tosses it into the trash can! Incredibly, he puts the box and the bow on his fireplace mantle. When visitors come to the house, he proudly shows them the box and the ribbon. He explains that the box once contained a precious diamond, but that he threw it away because he liked the wrapping better. His friends are

143

speechless and leave the house shaking their heads at the man's obvious lack of discernment."

Then, of course, I drove the point home: "The box in that story is the body, and the diamond is the soul. We take great pains to display the box to the world. We feed it, paint it, want it to be attractive at all times. But, sadly, we forget the diamond inside the box. We neglect the soul that is eternal and most precious. How foolish to spend all of our energy and attention on the box and neglect the diamond."

Now, as far as it goes, that illustration is true. For many in the "me" culture it is a needed word. It *is* tragic when we so accentuate the physical that we overlook the spiritual.

But that illustration perpetuates a fallacy that has been prevalent since the first century, namely that God is concerned about our soul and totally indifferent to our body. In every generation, it seems, there arises a group of Christians who propound the notion that God cares much about our "spiritual being" but nothing about our "physical being." The ancient Gnostics had this rigid body-soul dualism, and part of the New Testament was written specifically to refute it.

The New Testament clearly says that God is concerned about the totality of our being, not just some spiritual part encased in a physical shell. By all means, we must not neglect the diamond. But neither can we forget the box and bow either. According to no less an expert than the Apostle Paul, what we do with the box and bow is a crucial part of our Christianity:

> Do you not know that your body is a temple of the Holy Spirit, who is in you, whom you have received from God? You are not your own; you were bought at a price. Therefore honor God with your body (1 Cor. 6:19–20).

Another Lesson From the Past

The Gnostics saw life in sharp categories—black-white, divine-human, body-soul. Because they saw reality as a set

144

of "either/or's," they could not tolerate such orthodox contentions as Jesus being both divine and human. The idea that one person could be both God and man did not fit in their rigid mind set. A Gnostic might say, "Take your pick, Jesus was either divine spirit or human flesh. The two cannot co-exist."

Their dualism is still prevalent today. We still tend to think in "either/or" categories, and our compartmentalizing of life leads us away from truth. Like the Gnostics we draw a rigid line between *soma* (body) and *psyche* (spirit). Because we draw that line that separates us into a body and a spirit, we never see ourselves as we really are: *psychosomatic*, that is, body and spirit co-existing in one being. We never see that the doctor affects our attitude and the preacher our health.

If we err on the *soma* side—if we focus so much on the body that we neglect the spirit—we become those sad people who actually need to hear my tale about the box and the diamond. We become the intended recipients of Jesus' probing query: "What good will it be for a man if he gains the whole world, yet forfeits his soul? Or what can a man give in exchange for his soul?" (Matt. 16:26). I think one reason many of us are a little put off by the fitness fanatic, the fashion expert, and the cosmetics saleslady is our suspicion that they have tipped the scales so toward the body that they have forgotten the soul. If we opt only for care of the body, we become pretty, but empty, people.

But the other dualistic extreme is also devastating. If we err on the *psyche* side, we deny our humanity. Emerson once said, "Become first a good animal," but we modern Gnostics are repulsed by the idea. Prayer, Bible study, church attendance—this is our territory. After all, we're "spiritual." Diet, exercise, sleep—those are the world's concerns, and we're quite content if we're on the "spirit" side of the dualism to let the fitness buff and the egotist think of such things.

Obviously, both dualistic extremes are wrong. The

145

Gnostic way will not let us be what we are—both body and spirit, human beings created in the image of the divine. Let the "body" people begin to ponder the things of the soul, and they will be on the road to wholeness. Let the "spirit" people begin taking their bodies seriously, and they will be made complete as well. For only when we lovingly care for both *soma* and *psyche* can we become fully human.

The Physical Side of Faith

It is not unusual, is it, to see a devout Bible teacher who is an overweight glutton? Or a preacher who is tired all the time? Or a deacon with constant tension headaches? Or a "good Christian" with frequent colds? The only explanation for such phenomena is the Gnostic heresy: These sincere Christians see little connection between faith and fitness. Their view of Christianity demands that they worship, pray, and tithe. It does not so much as insinuate that they diet, exercise, or get more sleep.

If we deem ourselves an uptight Christian, we would do well to pay closer attention to Emerson. "Become first a good animal" is not such bad advice when undertaking a battle with stress. It is true that our nerves can wreak havoc on our bodies, but it is equally true that our bodies can wreak havoc on our nerves. Long-term neglect of the body always has destructive implications for the soul.

A Simple Course in Degeneration

Periodically, there will appear in print a story about some old man celebrating, say, a hundredth birthday. When asked about the secret of his longevity, the old man will wryly attribute it to good cigars, strong liquor, and loose women. We're left with the impression that we can choose any habits we wish and still live long, happy lives. I would not for a moment question the old man's story.

I would just remind you that his story is an aberration.

Most men who opt for cigars, liquor, and women will die long before their time. There was once a ballplayer who made the major leagues even though he had only one arm. However, I would not recommend, if you harbor dreams of the majors, that you amputate. One man might occasionally beat the odds. Most of us won't.

Actually, what we have to do to let our bodies degenerate is nothing. Nothing at all. It is the easiest thing in the world to abuse our bodies. We don't even need cigars, liquor, and wild women. All that is required is consistent neglect.

I recently heard a country tune on the radio that underscored for me the tragedy of neglect. The singer was wailing about a love gone sour. He tries, in the song, to figure out where he went wrong: He didn't lie, cheat, or physically abuse his woman, and is perplexed over her leaving. Then it dawns on him—"It's not what I did; it's what I didn't do." He finally sees why the relationship unraveled: He didn't hold her enough or tell her how much he loved her. The relationship withered from neglect. Neglect will kill a body just as it will kill a relationship.

The foolproof formula for *unfitness* has three simple words: "Don't do anything." Don't exercise. Don't control your habits. Don't monitor your sleep. Don't step on the scales. Don't watch what you eat. Don't check your blood pressure or cholesterol level. Don't see your body as a precious gift of God. Don't do anything about your body and it will become a wreck and ruin without fail.

Last spring, I planted a vegetable garden in my back yard. I planted peas, okra, tomatoes, cucumbers and squash and couldn't wait for the harvest. Unfortunately, I got busy with other things and neglected my own little plot. I promise you I did nothing sinister to my vegetables. I didn't cut them, or scream at them, or strip their leaves. I just did nothing. I let nature run its course, and hoped to savor fresh vegetables without lifting a finger to water, weed, or fertilize. How many vegetables do you suppose I harvested?

If we don't tend our bodies, the results will be all too predictable. We will reap a bumper crop of lethargy and frazzled nerves. Very few of us "uptight Christians" will actively abuse our body. We will never smoke or drink to excess, take drugs, or in any other way inflict overt damage to our body. We might, however, allow ourselves to quietly sag into *un*fitness.

Body Types

A good place to begin is with an awareness of body types. Before you go on a crash diet, or start lifting weights, or launch a running program, it would be wise to ascertain what kind of body you have.

Over thirty years ago, psychologist William Sheldon developed a system for classifying body types. He pinpointed people in three categories: The *endomorphs*, with predominantly soft, rounded muscles; the *mesomorphs*, with hard, strong muscles and big bones; the *ectomorphs*, with stringy muscles and slender, small bones.

Each of these body types, Sheldon asserted, manifests different psychological traits. In his view, the *soma* greatly affects and determines the *psyche*.

The endomorphs love people and social events. They tend to be relaxed, kind, generous, and cheerful. Endomorphs love comfort, are dependent on others for emotional security, and typically "let things happen." They are "the talkers."

Mesomorphs are dominant, assertive, and confident. They are also quick-tempered, reckless, and brimming with energy. These muscular people thrive on action and typically "make things happen." They are "the doers."

Ectomorphs love privacy and detachment. They are gentle, reflective, and reserved. The emphasis in their lives is on perceiving, and they typically "watch things happen." They are "the thinkers."

I imagine most of us are a mixture of those three types,

but probably we can see the one body temperament classification that best fits us. I am always suspicious of labels and categories, but it seems to me that Sheldon's theory is amazingly perceptive.

Those three types actually live in different worlds, enjoy different activities and relate to people in different ways. If we never come to grips with who we are, physically and emotionally, we will continually tune in on the wrong station for news about life. Dr. George Sheehan writes:

> Daily we endomorphs, mesomorphs and ectomorphs ignore these differences, and insist on asking other people how things are in our own private, personal, never-to-be-duplicated worlds. We are told the absolute, immutable truth in sports, politics, religion and art by people who never warn us: "Your world or ours, Finnegan?" These same people guide us into mess after mess. We find ourselves at a play we dislike, a movie we can't stand, reading a book that puts us to sleep or secretly enjoying a game that others consider a waste of time.

Our task, I think, is to get acquainted with who we are so that we can better know what God wants us to become. We have been designed with a unique pattern, a pattern that demands specific care and singular attention. To tune in on somebody else's music is a sure way to miss our own, never-to-be-repeated calling.

A Look in the Mirror

Walk, then, to the mirror and notice what you see. As I look at my own reflection, I remember:

- This body fits the ectomorphic category best. The psychological traits that Sheldon listed for the small-boned and stringy-muscled species are right on target for me—shy, private, reflective, loves to play with ideas. I see some of myself in the other two body types, but overwhelmingly I'm an ectomorph.
- This body has loose cartilage in its left knee, Mor-

149

ton's toe, a slightly sunken chest, a receding hairline, weak eyes, too much strain on its face.

- This body cannot tolerate roller coasters, merry-go-rounds, or even small cars on long trips. It gets nauseated easily.
- This body needs eight hours of sleep nightly. If it doesn't get its nightly quota, it makes the man who lives in it irritable.
- This body loves food. It does have an aversion, however, to liver, yogurt, hot peppers, and buttermilk.
- This body is more addicted to caffeine and sugar than it should be.
- This body hurts in more places than it did ten years ago.
- This body is a fabulous gift of God that must be maintained with special care.

Of that list, perhaps the final item is the only one we share. I would not wish certain facets of my physical self on anyone, just as I would not wish some of my emotional traits on anyone. What matters most is that all of us go to the mirror and discover the miracle that awaits us there.

What also matters is that we pay close attention to what our body is telling us and then vow to heed its message. Then and only then are we ready for the diet, or the exercise program, or the addition of a daily nap.

Incarnational Faith

If nothing else, our trip to the mirror ought to remind us that what we see there is important to God. Those small muscles, that thinning hair, those spindly, white legs are gifts of God, gifts that enable us to have productive, joyful lives.

Christianity has always been an incarnational religion. God, our Book says, takes up residence in earthen vessels. Most supremely, of course, in Jesus of Nazareth. But also, now, in you and me. His Spirit takes up residence in this slight, ectomorphic frame. He takes up residence in your soft, rounded endomorphic body or your heavily muscled mesomorphic one. My body and yours are temples of the Holy Spirit, and if we don't tend the temple, it says volumes about our love for its Creator.

That, in a nutshell, was the Gnostic's problem. The Gnostics denied the incarnation. They could not fathom God stooping to become flesh. Their god was interested in "religious" things; he gave no thought to "human" things.

When we neglect our body, we have fallen headlong into the Gnostic trap. In reality, our faith is so one-dimensional, God is not Lord over anything but our "religious" insides. Until we extend the boundaries of His lordship to include our physical outsides, we can't honestly call Him Lord.

Go back to the mirror. Gaze at your body there. What you see is God's gift to you. What you make of what you see, as the old saying goes, is your gift back to God.

And never forget that, for the Christian, life is nothing less than a series of love-gifts to the Father. "Therefore honor God with your body."

For Reflection and Discussion

1. Did you grow up in a Christian environment that neglected the "physical part" of discipleship?

2. Do you think most modern Christians are dualists who draw a rigid line between the "spiritual" and the "secular"?

3. What specific things are you doing to take care of your body? Is your body degenerating from simple neglect?

4. Which of the three body types best fits you?

5. Think about your body. List several characteristics of your physical self that come to mind.
   1.
   2.
   3.
   4.
   5.
   6.

6. Do you need to give more attention to the physical side of faith? What, in particular, do you need to start (or stop!) doing?

7. Have you ever thought that your uptight condition could have physical roots? How much of your stress do you think is caused by the Gnostic trap?

*You will keep in perfect peace him whose mind is
steadfast, because he trusts in you.*

Isaiah 26:3

*"Heap on other men the gift of riches, but give to
me the gift of the untroubled heart."*

From an Ancient Poem

12

THE STARTING PLACE

*S*herry and I did something unusual a few weeks ago. We farmed the kids out to friends and had an "adventure." We borrowed a motorcycle from a man in the church, doffed helmets and took off piggyback through the countryside. We ended up at a seafood restaurant by the bay and gorged on shrimp, oysters, stuffed crab and other assorted delicacies. Then we fired up the motorcycle and made the twenty-mile trip home in fine fashion.

Those parishioners who might have caught a glimpse of us as we sped by perhaps wondered if we'd lost our sanity. Staid, stern, Baptist parson on a motorcycle? Prim and proper preacher's wife a "motorcycle mama"? What's this world coming to?

I only know that for us it was a wonderful experience. We needed to play the fool, act like kids, shed respectability for an afternoon and escape the pious pose we are always expected to assume. When I lie on my deathbed someday, I feel certain that my main regret will be that I preached too many sermons and took too few motorcycle rides.

155

In fact, I think I'm telling you of our adventure primarily because we have so few of them and I must gloat over one that we've had. I have been expert at worrying about the future, wondering how the kids will turn out, straining to meet the expectations of the congregation, meticulously computing the family finances and checking to make sure all the doors are locked before I go to bed. I have not been so adept at taking motorcycles trips, laughing at jokes, taking long naps, and fishing cold streams.

Learning to Loosen Up

But, then, no one ever told us that we Christians could be *too* tight. We were clearly warned—and justifiably so—that we could be too loose, that we could stumble into immorality and thwart the abundant life. But no one told us that we could also squash our joy by being too careful, too conventional, and too circumspect. We have known since Vacation Bible School that we shouldn't be loose. Only in mid-life do we learn, if we learn it at all, that we shouldn't be tight.

I have never done a scientific study on the subject, but my guess is that for most "serious Christians" tightness is a bigger problem than looseness. I am not naive to the fact that loose living has crept into the sanctuary. I know Christian people succumb to lust, drunkenness, adultery, embezzlement, and other common immoralities. Those preachers who call for repentance have a valid message. Certainly, a good many contemporary Christians need to shape up and cast off the works of darkness.

But for every "loose" saint among us, there are probably ten who are too "tight." For every Christian who has erred on the wild side of life, there are ten who have erred on the tame side. Sadly, for these respectable, uptight Christians, Jesus' promise of abundant life has yet to be claimed—and *never* will be until they really hear the Good News and begin to live in its freedom. Ironically, the hope for today's church may not be in "loose" Christians getting "tight," but in "tight" Christians loosening up to enjoy life and experience the peace Christ offers.

Unloading the Camel

I want you to know that if you and I are ever going to regain control of our life, we will have to know how to unload our camels. Let me explain.

Jesus once said that it is easier for a camel to go through the eye of a needle than for a rich man to enter the kingdom of God (Matt. 19:24). Behind that statement lies an interesting historical fact.

One of the gates in the ancient Jerusalem wall was called the "Needle's Eye Gate." It was a narrow gate, just wide enough for a camel, but not for its baggage. Merchants entering the city had to unload their saddlebags for inspection at this gate, and only when the camel was stripped of its load could man and beast enter Jerusalem. A fully loaded camel simply could not squeeze through the "Needle's Eye."

We all stand before the door of joyful living. It is, however, a narrow gate (Matt. 7:13), and to get in we have to unload the camel. We have to strip off all of those encumbrances that won't allow us to enter. This book is actually a crash course on unpacking camels:

1. We can shed conformity and know that the popular way leads *away* from peace.

2. We can get rid of our mistaken notions about God and know that He is *for* us.

3. We can strip off our laziness, apathy and left-brain analytical thinking and begin to create—to use our God-like power to make new things.

4. We can remove unnecessary items from our budgets and make sure we are not possessed by our possessions.

5. We can simplify our activities and make certain our calendars are not crammed with "good" things.

6. We can eliminate our carelessness and busyness and begin to fill "love tanks"—to tend our relationships.

7. We can take off our false ideals and reconstruct our life maps.

8. We can shed our pretense and rid ourselves of that fake spirituality that destroys our relationships with God and people.

9. We can get rid of our guilt by learning from it and letting it teach us about the cross.

10. We can remove our other-worldly spirituality and begin to care for our bodies.

It seems to me that unless we get those ten things off the camel, we will have a hard time squeezing through the gate. I would like to think this book can at least be a starting place, that it can remind all of us that overloaded, un-tended camels can never enter the Holy City of Joyful Living.

Let It Begin in Me

The Hopi Indians had a fine word for which we have no equivalent in our language—*koyaanisqatsi*. The word can best be translated "life out of balance." The Hopis believe that life is supposed to be lived with a certain harmony and symmetry. When a person's life gets out of balance, that person has the dreaded condition known as *koyaanisqatsi*.

We have dozens of different words to try to express what the Indians expressed in that one word. We speak of anxiety, stress, misery, unfulfillment, burnout, boredom, tiredness. But the root problem is that lives are out of balance and need to be put back in line.

A popular old gospel song implores God to send a revival. The final line of the chorus begs—"And let it begin in me." I think of a line in a John Fowle novel, *Daniel Martin*, "I think she's trying to solve the world's problems as a substitute for facing one or two of her own." Renewal, in the best sense of the word, comes when we take aim at one or two problems of our own.

But, remember, the spiritual journey, the journey to eternal peace and joy, does have a price tag. In *The Road Less Traveled*, M. Scott Peck says:

> The journey of spiritual growth requires courage and initiative and independence of thought and action. While the words of the prophets and the assistance of grace are available, the journey must still be traveled alone. No teacher can carry you there. There are no pre-set formulas. Rituals are only learning aids, they are not the learning. Eating organic food, saying five Hail Marys before breakfast, praying facing east or west, or going to church on Sunday will not take you to your destination. No words can be said, no teaching can be taught that will relieve spiritual travelers from the necessity of picking their own ways, working out with effort and anxiety their own paths through the unique circumstances of their own lives toward the identification of their individual selves with God.

Spiritual growth takes effort. We have to keep unloading that camel if we want to get through the gate. But peace and joy are our rewards, and the effort is the best coinage we will ever spend.

Grace to you—and peace. May you learn in time how to whoop it up. In eternity, let's plan to have a ball together!

For Reflection and Discussion

1. How long has it been since you had an "adventure"? What is keeping you from having one?

2. Do you agree that "tightness" may be a bigger problem among contemporary Christians than "looseness"?

3. Which of the ten factors outlined in the book are causing your stress? What specific baggage do you need to unload from your camel before you can get through the gate of abundant living?

4. How do you reconcile the idea that spiritual growth is hard work with the idea that salvation comes completely through grace?

5. List below the specific things you need to do to stop being an "uptight Christian."
   1.
   2.
   3.
   4.
   5.